Demanding the Impossible

Demanding the Impossible

Slavoj Žižek

Edited by Yong-june Park

polity

First published in 2013 by Polity Press
Reprinted in 2013, 2014 (twice)

Polity Press
65 Bridge Street
Cambridge CB2 1UR, UK

Polity Press
350 Main Street
Malden, MA 02148, USA

ISBN-13: 978-0-7456-7228-1
ISBN-13: 978-0-7456-7229-8(pb)

A catalogue record for this book is available from the British Library.

Typeset in 11 on 14 pt Sabon by
Servis Filmsetting Ltd, Stockport, Cheshire
Printed and bound in Great Britain by T.J. International, Padstow, Cornwall

The publisher has used its best endeavours to ensure that the URLs for external websites referred to in this book are correct and active at the time of going to press. However, the publisher has no responsibility for the websites and can make no guarantee that a site will remain live or that the content is or will remain appropriate.

Every effort has been made to trace all copyright holders, but if any have been inadvertently overlooked the publisher will be pleased to include any necessary credits in any subsequent reprint or edition.

For further information on Polity, visit our website: www.politybooks.com

Contents

Contents

Acknowledgments

This book began as a part of the Global Humanities Project of Indigo Sowon, an educational center in Busan, South Korea. Founded in 2004, Indigo is a combination of book publisher, magazine, and bookstore, and also hosts international conferences. It seeks to provide a progressive, humanistic counterweight to the educational establishment, and to be an oasis of idealism and engagement (indigoground.net).

My first thanks are to the team of colleagues whose vision and hard work have made this project happen: Aram Hur, Youn-yeong Lee, Han-kyeol Yoon, Jin-jae You, and Dae-hyun Park, as well as Brian Palmer of Uppsala University (brianpalmer.org). I am immensely grateful to Slavoj Žižek, who invited our large team into his home over the course of two days. He is a person of astonishing energy and warmth, and we were left feeling that whatever his mind touches is electrified and made luminous.

My colleagues and I hope that the conversations in this book will prove enjoyable to the reader, and will spark lively discussions.

Yong-june Park

I

Politics and Responsibility

What is to be done for politics today? In the midst of radical changes – ecological catastrophes, fateful biogenetic mutations, nuclear or similar military-social conflicts, financial fiasco, etc. – where our commons are at stake, is there such a thing as the common good? To what extent is it useful to speak of the common good?

SŽ: For me, what is problematic is not the word "common" but the word "good." Because the way I see it, from my European perspective, traditional aesthetics was directed toward some *supreme Good*. It could be God, humanity, the universe, etc.: we see this *common good* as a supreme substantial value that we should all have to work for. But for me, modernity begins with Descartes, and then with Kant – to be precise, with an ethics that is no longer an ethics of the common good. For example, in Kant, you find it is purely formal ethics: ethics of the moral law and so on. Here, ethics cannot be, in any way, *politicized*: politicized in the sense that you cannot simply presuppose some common good.

Rather, it is a matter of decision. This is what I find problematic about the notion of the common good.

What is a common good today? OK, let's say ecology. Probably most people would agree, even though we are politically different, that we all care about the earth. But if you look closely, you will see that there are so many ecologies on which you have to make so many decisions. Having said that, my position here is very crazy. For me, politics has *priority* over ethics. Not in the vulgar sense that we can do whatever we want – even kill people and then subordinate ethics to politics – but in a much more radical sense that what we define as our good is not something we just discover; rather, it is that we have to take *responsibility* for defining what is our good.

And, as many radical ecologists have pointed out, how much of ecology, which pretends to work for the good of nature, involves *hidden* political choices? When you say, for example, that the common good should be our Mother Earth, and that our planet should thrive – why should our planet thrive? Because we humans want it to, so that we can survive. Ecology, from my point of view, is the most egotistic, human-centered machine there is. Nature is crazy. Nature is chaotic and prone to wild, unpredictable and meaningless disasters, and we are exposed to its merciless whims – there is no such thing as Mother Earth. In nature, always, there are catastrophes, things go wrong, and sometimes a planet explodes.

What I want to show you is the fact that, if you look at this closely, when we refer to some higher common good, it is always, at least the way I see it, defined by our secret priorities. For example, people may say "Oh! We are constructing another big city and it will destroy nature. It is horrible!" And the usual response to this, even of many ecologists, is that "we should live in a more natural way, closer to the forest, and so on." No! One ecologist, a friend of mine from Germany, whom I appreciate very much, told me that this kind of response is, ecologically, totally catastrophic. From an ecological standpoint, the best thing is this: there is a lot of pollution everywhere, so you pack as many people as you can into a big city; it is then very concentrated and there is much less pollution per capita so you can keep the large domains relatively clean. I don't know if you are doing this in Korea, but somebody told me they are doing it in Japan. I think that large dirty cities where people live packed together are ecologically the best thing for nature. Again, there is another ecological idea, as we call it, which is that we should live in small self-sufficient houses with solar energy – people believe this is one way of living ecologically. But can you imagine how it would end up if the majority of people wanted to live like that? Everyone would be very spread out, and the forests would disappear. Ironically, this is related to the question of how much we can "safely" pollute our environment. So I am very distrustful of this view. Whenever something is proposed as being for the higher good, and we say we should transcend our egotism and work for it, we will always discover that we are already secretly doing just this.

What I like to suggest, based on my basic position, is not politics in the sense of what people usually associate with politics – such as cheap manipulation, corruption, power struggles, etc. – but politics in the sense of fundamental decisions about our life on earth, and collective decisions for which you have to take *full* responsibility.

2
Obsession for Harmony/ Compulsion to Identify

What do you mean by "full responsibility"? If the common good is a matter of decisions we have to make, precisely in the field of political struggle and ecological crisis, is this a term that embraces responsibility even for social reform or revolution?

SŽ: Well, what I think problematic from a European perspective is this oriental wisdom that says there is some kind of natural balance or harmony of the elements. I don't see any harmony in this world. On the contrary, I see that all harmony is only *partial harmony*. What do I mean by this? Some people, for example, would say: "Communism was bad because it was too socializing. Everything was social, and no individuality was allowed. On the other hand, liberal capitalism is too individualistic and everybody is for himself, and so on. So they say they are both disharmonious, and we need a kind of middle road: a society that has a certain social sense of community but allows, nonetheless, some individual freedom." No! I think that what we should think about is this very *contrast*. How do we imagine individual freedom? And how do we imagine the common good? These questions already belong to a certain field. These are the extremes within that certain field. The first thing I would like to do is show how absurd it is to urge that we have two extremes and need to find the balance. These two extremes already flow into each other. This is why "synthesis" does not affirm the identity of the extremes, but, on the contrary, affirms their difference as such. So the *synthesis* delivers difference from the "compulsion to identify." In other words, the immediate passage of an extreme into its opposite is precisely an index of our submission to the *compulsion to identify*.

I can think of an example from North Korea. I read a book about North Korea, written by a Western author who was trying to describe the everyday life of the terrible hunger experienced there in the last 15 years – you know, when, 15 years ago, the North Korean state government simply more or less stopped functioning. That is to say, the state controlled pretty much every social infrastructure, so people didn't get enough food to survive and couldn't get a job, and so on. And what did emerge there? A kind of very rudimentary brutal form of capitalism: people went to the forest and gathered fruits for their own use and to sell at the market. Isn't it interesting how you find a terrible Darwinian survivalist individualism beneath everything – lavish spectacle, the Mass Games with their doll-like robotic dancers – that they show to the world? Basically, life for everyone is just for the individual. It was the same in Stalinism. Even in China, I claim that the real result of the Cultural Revolution is the capitalism that they now have.

On the other hand, look what we have in capitalism. People talk about individualism, but what kind of individualism is this? No wonder large corporations are delighted to accept such evangelical attacks on the state, when the state tries to regulate media mergers, put strictures on energy companies, strengthen air pollution regulations, protect wildlife, and limit logging in the national parks, etc. It is the ultimate irony of history that radical individualism serves as the ideological justification of the unconstrained power of what the large majority of individuals experience as a vast anonymous power, which, without any democratic public control, regulates their lives.

Let's see what is now happening on the internet. We get, more and more, to serialize our lives: we go to see the same movies and we watch the same news. People describe it as movement toward the clouds: cloud computing. We no longer need a big computer to play video games, like the one I have in my room to have fun with my son. A decade ago, a computer was a big box on one's table, and downloading was done with floppy disks and USB sticks; today, we no longer need strong individual computers, since cloud computing is internet-based – i.e., software and information are provided to computers or smartphones on demand, in the guise of web-based tools or applications that users can access and use through a browser as if it were a program installed on their own computer. In this way, we can access information from wherever we are in the world, on any computer, with smartphones putting this access literally into our pocket.

Everything happens out there. Are people aware of how this will standardize everything? We will only be connected to one single provider, like Google or iTunes, but we are limited to their choices. Our struggle should thus focus on those aspects that pose a threat to the transnational public sphere. Part of this global push toward the privatization of the "general intellect" is the recent trend in the organization of cyberspace toward so-called "cloud computing."

So back to the point: I don't like this approach which says that we have two extremes and we have to find a balance, because this principle, for me, is too abstract. For example, we may say that some countries have no democracy and, on the other hand, some have too much democracy. You can always say that we need balance. But the real revolution, for me, is when you change the balance itself: *the measure of balance.*

When I was very young, before the sexual revolution, it was considered that there were two different views: conservatives, who thought sex should be allowed only in marriage and, on the other hand, those who urged liberating sexuality. But what then happened? The balance totally changed. You cannot simply say that the old balance was lost and that we now have too much sexual freedom, but rather you should say that the very measure of what is extreme has changed. So for me this is the true revolution. It is that *totality* changed; the very measure of the extremes changed.

This is also related to your other question about social reform. The point is not that I think we need violence for social revolution. Of course I don't like violence. But for me reform means changes *within* the existing order: you can say that we now have too much individualism, so we need more social responsibility. But this stays within the field. On the contrary, revolution is where the basic rule of society changes. This is why capitalism was a radical revolution. Because the whole notion of stability has changed with capitalism or even with capitalistic democracy: only with capitalism does a certain dynamics became a part of stability. If things don't change, they fall apart. Capitalism changed the whole logic of social space. When you talk about stability today, it means the stability of dynamic development. It is a totally different logic of stability from that of pre-modern times.

3
Politicization of Ethics

How should we comprehend our responsibilities when faced with this new logic of modern capitalism?

SŽ: Well, I am suspicious about the notion of a common good. I think there is no common good, which is prescribed, a priori, in advance, by nature. Even with regard to nature, what would be the common good? We might say nature needs to be balanced so that humanity can survive on earth. But we will have to define the balance. I mean, as we all know, nature is crazy. Nature has catastrophes all the time. Can we even imagine what happened when dinosaurs died out or when oil was created? We know now that the Sahara Desert was once a large ocean.

So nature is not balanced. Here I am very modern. Before modernity, people believed, to put it very simply, in a predestined order: that is, a kind of global harmony which we humans have ruined, so now we have to return to it. I don't believe in this solution, especially with regard to ecology today. I don't think there is any natural order. Natural orders are catastrophic.

To return to your questions, I am, in this sense, in favor of the *politicization of ethics* in the sense that we are not only responsible for doing our duty or for working for the good, we are also responsible for deciding what this good is. Well, even when some people urge that there is a sort of natural balance, isn't this also a totally coherent *politico-ecological* decision? For example, some may say that the global population has grown too large – that there are too many people and we have developed too many productive forces, and so on. The point they make is that we should instead encourage infectious diseases so that at least two-thirds of humanity will die, while those who don't should learn to live more modestly. This will be best for the earth and even for humanity. I, of course, totally disagree with this vision, but what can you say a priori against it? You cannot argue from an ecological standpoint. What will you say? Is it bad for the earth? No! It's probably better for the earth than to say there should be food for all the people now living. Wouldn't the best thing for the earth be to organize slowly so that two-thirds of the people will die? For the earth, this is probably the best thing that could happen.

Here is my point. We already made some *ethico-political* decisions. This is what I would like to emphasize: we are much more free and responsible than we think. Usually it is fashionable to say – old Marxists used to say things like this – that "we just appear to be free. You go to the store and buy whatever you want, but in reality you are manipulated." It's true, but we are also way more free than we think we are. If you believe in some kind of a destiny, it makes life easier. The difficult thing is to break destiny. We all assume that this explosion of development and industry is our destiny. Even the majority of ecologists argue about how to make industry ecological. They accept the primacy of industry. But I find all this problematic.

I think the first step is to accept the consequence of modernity, which is radical freedom not only in the good sense, but also in the terrifying sense that we have to decide. It's totally up to us. This is what Jacques Lacan means when he says: "There is no big Other – *il n'y a pas de grand Autre.*" There is no agency on which we can rely. Whenever there is a crisis, people spontaneously look for some kind of a lost balance. All this started with Confucius, whom I think of as the original form of idiot. Confucius was not so much a philosopher as a proto-ideologist: what interested him was not metaphysical truths but, rather, a harmonious social order within which individuals could lead happy and ethical lives.

No wonder that Confucius' description of the disorder he sees in society around him ironically provides a good description of a really democratic society. Confucius proposes here a kind of proto-Althusserian theory of ideological interpellation: the ideological "big Other" (tradition), embodied in its apparatuses (rituals), interpellates individuals, and it is up to the individual to live and act in accordance with the title that makes him what he is. Confucius' idea was that crisis happens when the original harmony is lost and then the idea is to restore harmony. I think that we should drop this. There is no harmony to which we should or can return. For harmony, we have to *decide* what we want and we have to struggle and fight for it.

4
Means Without End: Political Phronesis

What kind of values should we foster to help guide our ethico-political decisions?

SŽ: What fascinates me are the events going on in Egypt. The West has been saying for years that "we want Arabs to become democratic." This is all hypocrisy. Now we have had a democratic explosion, which involved, at the same time – at least till now – absolutely no Muslim fundamentalism. Nonetheless everybody is afraid. This is what always fascinates me. Here, theoretical analysis begins and this is often true in politics: you bridge something from very different sides.

In Slovenia, we have a proverb that, if you talk too much, you want something: you really are afraid that something could happen and you talk a lot to make sure that it doesn't. It's a little bit like this with democracy in Arab countries. Everybody was saying that they needed democracy, but everyone was deadly afraid that democracy would finally come about there.

This is maybe where you should teach me. When you say common good, I think of something like true political activity – and of course I don't mean power struggle or corruption; rather, I mean the process of decision-making. In this political domain of judgments and decisions, we need what Aristotle called *phronesis*, a reflection, where you don't have any advanced theoretical measure and cannot determine your priorities in a non-political way. Politics for me is not just a means to make decisions on religious, social, and ethical issues in an objective way. It simply is not true.

The lesson of politics is that you cannot distinguish between *means and ends (goals)*. We all know this was the big contradiction of Stalinism. They wanted communist freedom, but the way they went about it achieved the opposite. So again, for me, politics precisely means that everything is a matter of decision-making, not that you have this self-willful contingent decision. But decisions are to be made, especially today and not only with ecology, but also with biogenetics and all other issues.

It is clear that we have to decide everything. In a very short period of time, we will be able to do horrific things that not only influence physical appearances, by manipulating genes, but that also influence psychological properties. For example, a couple of years ago, I visited Beijing and Shanghai and met some people who were working for the Chinese Academy of Sciences, and they showed me a pretty horrifying program at their Institute of Biogenetics. They said: "Our goal is to take care of the physical welfare and also the *psychological* welfare of the Chinese people." This means that they plan somehow to control even the psychological properties of the people. Here, the old religion doesn't work. All our traditional wisdoms – you can't apply them here. Because the basic coordinates are undermined.

Traditional ethics tells us that one should do one's duty and work hard. But let me give an example of two students. One is lazy and the other works hard. In normal ethics, the good guy who works hard will win. But what if the lazy one takes some pills, which tremendously enhance his ability so that he then works just a little bit and beats the hard-working one? What will you do here? Will you prohibit pills? The ethical coordinates change here.

Jürgen Habermas – although I disagree with him – was aware of this, and his solution was simply not to do it. But I don't think his solution works. Can you imagine how painful a decision this is? Let's say I am a lazy student and you are a hard-working student. You work hard and I take a pill and do it much faster, without any effort, than you. Then you will have every right to feel like an idiot. Why did you have to go through all that ethical effort and hard work? What is the basis of our ethics? That you become free? As people like to say: "Freedom comes with duties. To be free you have to earn it by disciplining yourself and working hard." But what if we have to change the very discipline and the sense of work? What if it can be influenced through some chemical means, even genetics? Everything changes. So we are in a totally new situation.

So again, if what you mean by the common good is an awareness that we have to decide what the common good is, then I agree with you. I just don't believe that, with regard to where humanity is today, we still can apply the traditional Confucian paradigm that there is chaos so we should return to stability. We should decide what stability we want. And we don't have any guarantee of any natural balance or social harmony. In this respect, I am a pessimist.

5
"May You Live In Interesting Times"

Speaking of our strikingly new situation, you once quoted Antonio Gramsci: "The old world is dying away, and the new world struggles to come forth: now is the time of monsters." And in these interesting times, there is something right in front of us. Among all these so-called monsters, how do you analyze the rise of China, seen by some as the new monster?

SŽ: I don't know if this is true, but in Europe we claim that the Chinese have this proverb that if you really hate someone, the curse to fling at them is: "May you live in interesting times!" But when I was in China, they told me that they heard this from Western people. It's typical how you attribute something to some people and then if you go to them, they don't know anything about it. Somehow, historically, the "interesting times" have been periods of unrest, war and struggles for power in which millions of innocents suffered the consequences. And today we definitely live in interesting times – with danger and tensions.

Who knows what will happen with the growing chaos of nature and economics. This is what worries me: there have been big debates where some people started to doubt ecologists, claiming that they are just exaggerating global warming. But the point is just an easy answer: when you listen to the good ecological scientists, they warn that global warming doesn't simply mean that it will get warmer everywhere, it means there will be more extremes. There is a prediction, which is paradoxical, that if global warming continues, there may be a new ice age in Western Europe. It's a theory about the Gulf Stream: if it gets warmer, the Gulf Stream will no longer reach Europe. People tend to forget that New York is geographically at the same level as Spain. That is to say we, in Europe, have relatively warmer weather than people in the North. So global warming means a new ice age in Europe. This is madness.

Again, this is what I try to adhere to: given the sense of urgency, we need to think – and this is not because of any of my communist dreams. I have lived in a communist country. I know how horrible it was – in a more *global* sense. Let's say something like a new ice age in Europe or more severe droughts in Africa do happen. At the same time, they tell us – I don't know whether it's true – the gigantic forests in northern Siberia will become habitable because the permafrost is melting there. True, climate change will bring increased competition for resources, coastal flooding, infrastructure damage from melting permafrost, stresses on animal species and indigenous cultures of the region – all this accompanied by ethnic violence, civil disorder, and local gang rule. In the same way, we hear more and more voices enjoining us to heed global warming.

The pessimistic predictions should be put into a more balanced context.

But if this happens, do we even have mechanisms to organize things? How will we transfer people from, let's say, Africa to wherever? There are already spontaneous transfers happening. In a year or so, cargo ships will be able to take a direct northern route, cutting the consumption of fuel and reducing carbon emissions. And I was told that many Chinese are already moving to Siberia. Are we aware of what is happening? Two million Chinese are already in Africa taking over. This horrifies my leftist friends there.

But I'm telling them that we are effectively approaching a multicentric world, which means we need to ask new, and for the traditional left, unpleasant questions. Doesn't this mean that maybe we should accept that the United States is not always automatically the bad guy? We talk about America being an economic neocolonialist state, but what about Chinese neocolonialism? I am what you might call abstractly an anti-capitalist. I am, for instance, suspicious of the old leftists who focus all their hatred on the United States. Why is the left silent about that? When I say this, it annoys them, of course. But it is obvious that China is now a mega economic colonial power in Africa. They are doing some better things than the West, but not all. For example, take Sudan or Zimbabwe where they are ruthlessly creating factories run by local tyrants. Or take Myanmar. It is absolutely clear how the General survived the great protest led by the Buddhist monks a couple of years ago: the military regime was saved with the discreet help of Chinese security advisors. Myanmar is effectively a Chinese economic colony, with China playing the standard postcolonial strategy of supporting the corrupt military regime in exchange for the freedom to exploit the vast natural resources.

It is the same as what South Korean business corporations tried to do in Madagascar. I've heard that it didn't go through, but it is another example of capitalist colonialism. As I was told, the plan was pretty horrible. Daewoo Logistics, one of the major international corporations in South Korea, announced that it wanted to buy some 3.2 million acres of farmland, the most fertile land, in Madagascar, amounting to nearly half of its arable land. And it plans to put about three-quarters of this land under corn, with the remainder used to produce palm oil, a key commodity in the global biofuels market. And they claim that their deal will also benefit Madagascar. But everyone knows that it is OK as long as the economy goes well. If not, people in Madagascar will suffer from hunger. I really think we are living in such crazy times, where, without some kind of links beyond and above the level of state, we will be lost in a new chaos. The circle of postcolonial dependence is thus closed again.

From what I heard from my political friends, many states are silently already preparing for debt. One way to read American politics is to see it based on the premise that most of the world will be in chaos soon. So we just have to isolate ourselves, protect ourselves and think about how we have control over a few vital issues, like oil in the Middle East. And the others – who cares? Let them starve. So communism is once again at the gates. Who is to decide on the priorities here, and how, if such decisions cannot be left to the market? It is here that the question of communism has to be raised once again.

6

Communism: The Ethico-Political Fiasco

As you have argued, the resuscitation of the notion of communism can only be justified when it is related to the commons. And in an interesting interview with the Guardian, *you "disclosed the secret" that communism will win. What did you mean by that? And by your claim that the explosion of uprisings and rebellions would lead us to overcome the failures of twentieth-century communism?*

SŽ: I like the aspect of *common*, in the sense that we are facing mega problems where old notions of sovereign states or even issues like ecology are being questioned. See, for example, what they did for the financial crisis: compare the $700 billion spent by the US alone in order to stabilize the banking system to the fact that, of the $22 billion pledged by richer nations to help develop poorer nations' agriculture in the face of the current food crisis, only $2.2 billion has so far been made available. The financial meltdown made it impossible to ignore the blatant irrationality of global capitalism. In this sense, the Copenhagen Climate Summit was simply a fiasco. When there is any type of ecological meeting, all they say is: "Yes, we should go on talking and then we succeeded because we decided that we will meet again and talk in two years." You see, nonetheless, for the financial crisis, they are able to act immediately with sums of money, which are simply unbelievably huge. This, I think, is a paradox.

Look what Stalin said: "If you shoot one person you are a murderer. If you kill a couple of persons you are a gangster. If you are a crazy statesman and send millions to their deaths you are a hero." It's horrible. We now can say the same thing about crime. If you steal one hundred thousand dollars, you are a thief. If you destroy billions, banks and the state will help you. I'm really worried.

This is what I mean about my communism – not the Leninist version, which was total madness. Many leftists hate me when I argue that twentieth-century communism might have been the biggest ethico-political fiasco in the history of humanity. I think there is no other soft explanation. Some things were done well here and there, but globally it was a fiasco. But the problems, to which communism tried to provide an answer, are still here, more than ever. They are returning.

This is why I like to say communism, for me, is not an answer. Communism is not the name of a solution but the name of a *problem*: the problem of the *commons* in all its dimensions – the commons of nature as the substance of our life, the problem of our biogenetic commons, the problem of our cultural commons ("intellectual property"), and, last but not least, the problem of the commons as that universal space of humanity from which no one should be excluded. Whatever the solution might be, it will have to solve this problem. So what you are trying to capture with the common good is the name of a problem. This is communism for me. What will be the answer? I don't know. Maybe we don't have an answer. Maybe it will be a catastrophe. Maybe . . . I don't know.

Nonetheless, and I'm not being too pessimistic here, but what shocks me, again and again, is how so-called specialists are proven wrong. About 10 or 15 years ago, people said that in postmodern times there are no longer revolutions; forget about people taking to the streets. My god, now you have them all around. Who knows where we will go from here?

I would like to see Saudi Arabia. This is the true worry. Everybody is in a panic not so much because of Egypt, but Saudi Arabia, which is an incredibly corrupt regime. But do you know what's really absurd? It is that corruption, in a way, doesn't exist there, because it is the system itself. In other countries you have politicians who steal from the state, but there the king *is* the state, so he doesn't have to steal. The system itself is simply horrible.

I was in Qatar for the New Year and I met some people from Saudi Arabia who told me this incredible story. Basically, the royal family possesses the state. They don't even have to steal anything, because they already have it. The key is that they all have a mistress and the breeding, so there are around 10,000 princes in the family. They all have a wonderful life. But if you go out into the neighborhoods, the country has its own poverty. Did you know that, a couple of years ago, there were small demonstrations even in Saudi Arabia? It has already started there. Now everyone is afraid in the

West, but don't they see that the more it is postponed, the more crazy and self-destructive the explosion will be?

I see explosions everywhere. In Qatar, a female curator at a museum took me to an industrial city in the suburb of Doha. I asked immediately who does the work for all those nice buildings. It seemed almost like a concentration camp. You have military barracks for immigrant workers. They just seem like self-employed men who sold themselves into slavery. Many of them came from Nepal, Indonesia, or the Philippines. And for four years, they take away the workers' passports and claim that it is a safe way to pay the stipend. They are not even free to leave. They have to work without air-conditioning where the temperature in summer rises to 57°C. Literally, in this temperature, if you step out you can fry eggs without any problem. And they are paid $150 per month out of which the company takes some for food.

Now comes the beauty: they want them to be *invisible*. On Friday, they are free to visit the city. But to prevent them from going to stores, they found an ingenious solution. Every Friday, entry into a shopping mall is prohibited to single men – officially, to maintain the family spirit in the malls; but this, of course, is only an excuse. Of course, all these workers are single. So under the pretext of protecting the family, they are prohibited from going to shopping malls on the only day they are free. This is all just waiting to explode. It's interesting what is happening in all these places – Qatar, Abu Dhabi, Dubai. This is slavery and it will just explode.

7
Who Is Afraid of a Failed Revolution?

We are now witnessing all these explosions, from Egypt to Tunisia. And what if they just end up as a mere revolutionary episode? In these economically stressed times, why is it that we are expanding the war, why is the US administration expanding the war in Afghanistan?

SŽ: What I always repeat is that the West itself created the problem here: this rise of religious fundamentalism is strictly an effect of the retreat of the left. You can see it, for example, in Afghanistan. Just 40 years ago Afghanistan was an extremely secular, tolerant Middle East Muslim country. There was a king who was a kind of pro-Western secular technocrat and a very strong local communist party. Then what happened? The communist party forced a *coup d'état* and the Soviet Union and the West intervened with Americans backing up the Muslim fundamentalists, so now we have fundamentalist Afghanistan. Isn't this a nice paradox? It is not an old traditional fundamentalist society that we should enlighten, but, in every way, it became entangled in world politics, which made it fundamentalist. With the global liberal system, we generated fundamentalism. It's the same in all Arab countries.

I claim that this rise of religious fundamentalism is strictly the other side of the disappearance of the secular left in Muslim countries. We tend to forget how strong the secular left was in the Arab countries. It played a pretty honorable role. It wasn't just an instrument of the Soviet Union in Syria, Iraq, or even in Egypt. And we all know, for example, what was probably the greatest crime of the Egyptian politician Gamal Abdel Nasser. In the mid-6os, he basically killed all the communists. I often quote Walter Benjamin, who said: "Every rise of fascism bears witness to a failed revolution." This is perhaps more pertinent today than ever.

Liberals like to point out similarities between left and right "extremisms": Hitler's terror and camps imitated Bolshevik terror, the Leninist party is today alive in al Qaida – yes, but what does all this mean? It can also be read as an indication of how fascism literally replaces (takes the place of) the leftist revolution: its rise is the left's failure, but simultaneously a proof that there was a revolutionary potential, dissatisfaction, which the left was not able to mobilize. Is the rise of radical Islamism not exactly correlative to the disappearance of the secular left in Muslim countries? Where did this secular tradition disappear? This should be our message to center liberals: "Ah, you got rid of us, the extreme left, and now you have religious fundamentalists."

If a *new secular left* does not emerge – I don't mean "revolutionary" in the sense of killing people, but I mean "revolutionary left" precisely in the sense of certain radical measures which could safeguard, as we would like to see it, the liberal legacy – we will find ourselves reaching what in Europe we ironically call "capitalism with Asian values," which means totalitarian capitalism.

We are approaching it now. Look at Italy, Hungary, or even Western Europe. We are seeing new forms of racism in Europe. Sweden is not so bad, but when I was in Norway they told me that even there the second party is already an anti-immigrant party. The Netherlands, a country that was always considered to be a symbol of tolerance, is also the same. This is very worrying. You cannot imagine what a strong hold authoritarianism is having in Hungary and how this is linked with the rehabilitation of fascism. The latest fashion of the European right, from Italy to Hungary to Romania, is to focus everything on Hitler, so that you can save others. The right wing say that they are totally against Nazism, not fascism. Say Mussolini was not so bad, and Franco was not that bad, but this is just to save the other soft fascists. Why this urge to save, not ex-functionaries of "soft" fascist regimes like the one in Italy itself, but Nazis themselves, whose ideology was explicitly anti-Christian, pagan? Well, I see so many problems with all this.

8
Another World Is Possible

It might have disappointed readers who wished to find an answer from your notion of communism. I also believe that the obligation of the secular left is not just to struggle for ideology but also to begin from the beginning, as you quoted Lenin at his Beckettian best, which brings about the big question. You once mentioned that the difficulty of today's capitalism is, in effect, that we cannot even imagine a viable alternative to global capitalism. Are we really not able to envision a possible alternative? What will be our only possible option? How do you picture the new model of a good society? What is your idea of the future? What sort of society do you want?

SŽ: If you ask me what will be our future, my model is this: did you see that wonderful film *Brazil* by Terry Gilliam? It came out almost 30 years ago, but it's a beautiful film, a totally crazy comedy, and it shows the future England under a totalitarian regime, but also with private hedonistic pleasure. It is not the dignified authoritarian way, but a kind of Groucho Marx in power. Isn't the first step of Berlusconi, a former prime minister of Italy, close to this? Also, in China, at the level of private life, no one cares about your private perversions, but just don't mess with politics. It is no longer the typical fascist mobilization. Liberal democratic capitalism is approaching its limit, and we need large, coordinated social actions. Otherwise the future will resemble the film *Brazil*.

I think that the new authoritarianism will not be like the old one within the discipline order, but it will result in a strange society where, at the consumerist and private level, you will have all your sexual freedom or whatever you want and, at the same time, you will have a kind of *depoliticized* order. It's a horrible thought. So how should we measure this?

Another meaning of common is very important in the context of common sense, common manners. This is why I like to shock people, telling them that I am in favor of authoritarian values. What do I mean by this? Let me give you an example. I wouldn't like to live in a state where you have to argue that it is not right to rape women. It's obscene. What kind of society is this where these values need to be debated? I would like to live in the society where there is no question that the very idea of rape is considered absolutely disgusting and crazy. And the same goes for racism, fascism, and so on.

The measure of ethical status in society depends not on certain things that are debated, but on certain things that are simply accepted as unwritten rules. For example, in Europe you don't get to see signs telling you, "Don't spit on the floor. Don't throw food around." I'm not being disparaging, but I was told that they have such signs in China. But in Europe it's automatically understood. You don't even have to write it on the wall. This is, I think, the *ethical standard* of society. Not what is explicitly prohibited or allowed, but what is to such an extent accepted that you don't even have to refer to it.

And if you look at Europe, standards are falling terribly. In this sense, things that were considered impossible 20 or 30 years ago are today becoming more and more acceptable. For example, 20 or 30 years ago, the very idea of having the extreme right in power was unacceptable. They were considered anathema: all the small neo-fascist parties, like Jörg Haider in Austria, Jean-Marie Le Pen in France. We didn't talk with them. We are in a democratic society, so we tolerate them. But it was absolutely out of the question to have them in power. But then this fell down. You now have them in Austria and elsewhere. They all of a sudden become respectable. The way we think of fascism: until now, it was a consensus in Europe that fascism is bad. But now you have debates about it. And, as I claimed, the same will happen more and more with racism.

The same thing happens even now apropos Egypt. I think that the West will increasingly have to abandon democracy – even if we hold on to some form of it. It will become more and more fashionable to say "Yeah, democracy. But you cannot apply it directly, some people are not mature enough." Israel already said this openly: "We support Mubarak because Egyptians are not yet mature people for democracy." But isn't it ironic? Because this revolution in itself proved that they wanted democracy.

I really think we are approaching potentially dangerously chaotic times. What I seriously see is a kind of *new authoritarian society* different from fascism. I don't like what many people claim, "Oh! It's a new fascism." I don't like this term, because what I claim is something new and I don't even like their use of the term in this metaphoric way where they appear to say something precise, but all they do is betray their lack of analysis. When people describe what's happening now in Hungary as fascism, basically they are saying: "I don't know what is happening, it just reminds me of what was happening 60–70 years ago." That's not good.

I think today the world is asking for a real alternative. Would you like to live in a world where the only alternative is either Anglo-Saxon neoliberalism or Chinese-Singaporean capitalism with Asian values? What I'm afraid of is that with this capitalism with Asian values, we get a capitalism that is much more efficient and dynamic than our Western capitalism. But I don't share the hope of my liberal friends. The marriage between capitalism and democracy is over.

The lesson of Wall Street for me is that the true utopia does not mean we can have a different society. The true utopia is the way things are, that they can go on indefinitely just like that. I claim that we are approaching some tough decisions. If we do nothing, then we are clearly approaching a new *authoritarian* order.

9

For They Know Not What They Do

Even though we are approaching potentially dangerous times of chaos and confronting tough decisions, we do not know what is really going to happen. How shall we deal with this time of uncertainty, of "the unknowns"?

SŽ: I really think we are living in very dangerous, interesting times. Everything is changing, including human nature itself, along with the prospect of bio-genetics, etc. I was always absolutely fascinated by this phenomenon of directly connecting our brain and physical activity without the use of apparatus. For example, when I was in New York, I saw on TV that crippled people in wheelchairs can control the movement just by their mind. You don't even need Stephen Hawking's proverbial little finger: with my mind, I can directly cause objects to move; that is to say, it is the brain itself that will serve as the remote-control machine. It is literally a realization of the Orwellian notion of "thought control." If you just *think* strongly about moving forward, the wheelchair moves forward.

Now this sounds very nice. We feel like we are God. We can move objects with our thoughts. But the problem here is that, first, if this can go on outside, it could also go on inside. This is to say, maybe someone could also control your thoughts from the outside. I mean what is clear is that our very sense of identity – "what are we?" – is based on this gap. This very gap between my thought and the world out there is the basic foundation of our senses of personal identity, where freedom is being undermined. We don't know what this means, what really is happening. We are entering such a new world. We don't know.

Some leftists like to say: "We know what is happening. But we just don't know how to mobilize people." No! For example, what is happening today in China? Is it simply an authoritarian form of capitalism? Is it a new form of communism? Is it something totally new? We have old Marxists and old liberals who agree about one thing, simply that the old form of communism is even more triumphant. But they don't have a good theory. We have many of these new slogans – postindustrial society, reflective society, postmodern society, information society – but I think these are just journalistic names. We don't yet know what is happening. So we need *theory* and *philosophy* more than ever.

Today is the *time for theory*. Why? Look at the debates about abortion and so on. You cannot simply apply old religious wisdom, because it is a totally new situation. Should we or should we not allow genetic research? Do you notice how confused the debates are? It totally shocked me how in Europe Catholics and Christians oppose biogenetic interventions, claiming that humans have an immortal soul, and they are not just machines, so we shouldn't mess with them. But I ask them a very naive question: If you believe that humans have an immortal soul, which is independent of matter, why then are you afraid of biogenetic interventions? They just take place in the brain; they cannot attack the immortal soul. We are all aware that we are touching on something that is very dangerous.

I don't think either of the standard solutions works. On the one hand, there is a conservative solution (Jürgen Habermas / the Catholic Church), which simply urges that this should be stopped, that it should be prohibited. It's dangerous to mess with it, so let's set up a limit. On the other hand, you have this man Ray Kurzweil, a main representative of techno-digital apocalypticism, an ultra-optimist, who says that we are moving to a stage of technological singularity, human species and its transmutation into the "post-human." Both are obviously wrong. There is hard work to be done. It is a unique task.

10

Parallax View on Postmodern Globalization

Can postmodernism tell us something about today?

SŽ: The good thing is – I may sound like a Eurocentric – that the Western world is losing its privilege. It's open to everyone. One thing I like about what we fashionably called postmodern society is that it no longer works with this sense of old status. Look at Singapore. About 60 or 70 years ago it was a backward village state. Now it's a state with maybe the highest income per capita. Generally, we think of Lichtenstein, with its banking system, as being one of the richest, but I think it lost its reputation during the financial crisis, while Singapore did very well. Even in the crisis of 2009, it grew by 15 percent. These are, and not just in a cynical way, the proofs of our interesting times. And it is a very good effect of postmodern capitalism that everyone is given a chance.

I don't even agree with those who claim that postmodernism means Americanization. No, postmodernism means that even in a small nation everyone gets a chance. This is why in Europe some people are against globalization. I think that the big victims of globalization are not the United States or China, but second-level traditional powers like France or Germany. Nobody even speaks their languages today. All my French friends are furious because 40 years ago English was considered vulgar and the true international language was French. Now nobody speaks it. Even English is a loser. I read a wonderful text claiming that what we are talking now, this English, which is emerging as the world language, is some sort of strange language that is actually very different from what is spoken in traditional English-speaking countries. The English language itself will, as a result of its global dominance, become lost. Some of the English that is being spoken somewhere in a Chinese market may well be more real than what English farmers are talking.

Do you know where I see good points here? Globalization is so amazing that I myself also even know about your Korean films. I even know that Taiwan films are now fashionable. Isn't this wonderful? The domain that I like very much is the detective novel. My god, now you have them everywhere! Today, there are detective series taking place in Native American reservations in the US, in the industrial Ruhr area of Germany, in Venice and Florence, in Iceland, in Brezhnev's or Yeltsin's Russia, even in today's Tibet (James Pattison's series with the Chinese police inspector exiled there for political reasons as a hero).

In Sweden, of course: they are the kings of the detective novel there. Stieg Larsson is a special case; he's not properly a detective novelist, but Henning Mankell definitely is. Mankell's true achievement is that, among today's writers, he is a unique artist of the *parallax*

view. That is to say, the two perspectives – that of
the affluent Ystad and that of Maputo (the capital of
Mozambique) – are irretrievably "out of sync," so that
there is no neutral language enabling us to translate one
into the other, even less to posit one as the "truth" of
the other. All we can ultimately do in today's conditions
is to remain faithful to this split as it stands and, in the
absence of any common denominator, to record it.

Let's take an absurd case: Arnaldur Indriðason in
Iceland. The whole country of Iceland has fewer than
300,000 inhabitants. Do you know how many copies of
his latest detective novel sold in Iceland? 50,000 copies.
It's like the Bible – every family has one. And he's selling hundreds of thousands in France, Germany, now
also in English. Reykjavík City even offers a literary bus
tour that focuses on the crime novels of Indriðason. Just
like the Mankell tour in Ystad. This is the good side of
postmodernism, for me. You couldn't even imagine all
this 40 years ago. We live in such interesting times, with
great dangers, but also with hopes.

And the rules are changing. It's quite incredible to
see the structure of Hollywood. Many foreign actors,
directors, and cameramen are able to work there. For
example, there, in Hollywood, are Miroslav Ondříček,
a Czech cinematographer, and Vilmos Zsigmond, who
is one of the most influential Hungarian-born cinema-
tographers in history. The good thing about Hollywood
is that, in contrast to what others think, it is much more
open to the world. I also like Chinese mega spectacle
films like *Hero*, *House of the Flying Daggers*, *The Curse
of the Golden Flower*, and so on. The Chinese are
now making better historical spectacle movies than the
Americans. They are making the best.

In a way, I like to see how things are really changing. I think, in the long term, globalization does not mean we will all eat hamburgers; globalization means that a true *global field* will emerge. I think that the United States will slowly lose their priority. They make few big hits, but even Russia is emerging with interesting major historical spectacles. And Korea and even Romania too. You see, this is what I like to emphasize about the postmodern era.

11

The Public Use of Scandal

One of the critical analyses about postmodern society is the fact that our private life is being threatened or is even disappearing. Even though the descriptions of postmodern times, like the "Risk Society" or the "Information Society," are misused as journalistic slogans, it is somehow true that individuals are deprived of their privacy and also of their right to public life.

SŽ: What I'm claiming is that something strange is happening. In some Western countries and in the United States, you can be a total creep or a complete idiot – there is no limit – but you can still be a leader. For example, Clinton: we all know, or at least surmise, that he did it. The majority of people believe there was something between the two of them; they believe that Clinton was lying when he denied it. Nonetheless, they support him. So everything can be open; there is no limit. You can say all this and everything still functions. In a way it designates the key element of the efficiency of an ideological statement or of a power structure.

This power structure is totally cynical. "Say whatever you want! It will happen anyway." This is also a very dangerous cynical tendency. And all big "public issues" are now translated into attitudes toward the regulation of "natural" or "personal" idiosyncrasies.

The next step is Berlusconi. He has been accused of prostitution and cheating, but he's still at the top in Italy. When people claim that everything is open to the media and we no longer have a private life, I claim, on the contrary, that we no longer have a *public* life. What is effectively disappearing here is public life itself, the public sphere proper, in which one operates as a symbolic agent who cannot be reduced to a private individual, to a bundle of personal attributes, desires, traumas, and idiosyncrasies. The public domain is fast disappearing and we treat it as a private domain.

I was shocked when a German former Foreign Minister, Joschka Fischer, an old leftist, after being charged with relaxing controls on visa regulations for Ukraine and allowing illegal immigrants with fake identities, explained his decision on public television. It was like watching some sort of TV reality show like *Actor's Studio*. He said, "I had a bad night. I was thinking and I was crying." My god, we are talking about dignified *public* decisions. We don't care about his private traumas and worries. It doesn't matter.

Do you know who started this shameless openness? The US President Richard Nixon. I sympathize with him more and more. I think he should be rehabilitated. Forget about the ideology of two journalists overthrowing him. It is clear that there must have been some support in the US establishment. This is the myth of US democracy: "Look what a great country we are.

Two ordinary journalists, Woodward and Bernstein, can overthrow a president." But what I'm saying is that Nixon was the last one to struggle with dignity. He wanted to be dignified, but he couldn't. He was a crook, but a crook who fell victim to the gap between his ideals and ambitions and the reality of his acts, and who thus experienced an authentically tragic downfall. What a tragic case.

But Ronald Reagan was totally a new model, who shamelessly displayed his deficiencies and weaknesses: a so-called "Teflon" president whom one is tempted to characterize as post-Oedipal – a "postmodern" president. I remember all the stupid liberal media people who, after every speech of Reagan, published a long report enumerating all the mistakes he made. Do you know what people discovered? The more he was caught making stupid mistakes, the more popular he became. People simply identified with this false "humanization."

Berlusconi is doing this masterfully. People don't want a perfect leader, they want a leader with weaknesses like them, even with vulgarities. I read a nice analysis of Berlusconi: what it said is that he is just like an average Italian. He wants to screw around with women and he wants to cheat with taxes. They have a president who perfectly embodies or enacts the mythical image of the average Italian. People identify with him and he still remains popular. And yet, this appearance of his being "just an ordinary guy like the rest of us" should not deceive us.

What I wanted to say through all of this is that something very important is changing – I don't know how to formulate it – in the way that political leaders operate today. I claim that this old figure of a masterful leader with dignity is disappearing. Even Putin is very careful about this tendency. At some charity event, Putin played the piano and sang "Blueberry Hill." I asked my friend, who is close to Putin, and he said that it is all planned, in the same way that he appears to lose his nerve and, from time to time, use dirty words. He knows this makes him popular. Something is changing here even with the features of the new model of political leader.

12

The Screen of Politeness/ Empty Gestures and Performatives

How do you understand the general analysis of North Korea?

SŽ: If you ask me about North Korea, I think it is interesting, as an extreme case, to ask how this regime functions; how it is possible. From what I read, one or two years ago North Korea changed its constitution, dropping out all references to socialism and communism. It is now some kind of patriotic military regime. Also what interests me is that even when Mao Zedong and Stalin were still in power and local media were praising them, North Korea never *directly* upheld the supernatural. At that time, it never claimed that Mao could create wonders, but now that is what is said in North Korea.

For example, the official story of the death of Kim Il-Sung is that, when he died, thousands of ravens came down because people cried so much, so they decided not to take his soul away. It's very interesting how the first communist regime directly transformed into supernatural dimensions. What intrigues me is a very simple question: do ordinary people in North Korea believe it or not? The answer might be relatively complex, because in a way they might not believe it, but, in another way, they cannot be simply cynical. There must be an interesting self-blinding confused mechanism.

I wonder how much the floodgates will open. I read somewhere that they are now getting more cellphones and DVDs smuggled in from China. Will the regime survive with this? And if they want unification, what will happen if it takes place all of a sudden? My God, there are 20 million poor people. Are outsiders allowed to visit North Korea? I was told that you could go into North Korea via China, and in Beijing there are some agencies through which to do this. Recently I was told that the only way to visit there was either officially, as a diplomat or journalist, or you have to become a member of some North Korean Society of Friendship and play along with it for at least two years. I like this: even in the worst days of Stalinism, you were prohibited from talking with foreigners, and in North Korea I read that it's even very dangerous for local people if you fix your gaze on them or if they have any kind of communication, even a non-verbal one too, with a foreigner.

The problem is if North Korea collapses; we don't want a repeat of the mistakes made in the case of East Germany. If you ask me, it might sound horribly somehow fascist or totalitarian, but I wouldn't open the border immediately. What would happen if the North were to collapse immediately? Practically, it would be too dangerous and chaotic. I'd retain North Korea as a kind of special zone and gradually solve problems. I'm not a *utopian*. Here I'm very realistic. Because West

Germany made a mistake: they just threw an incredible amount of money into East Germany – as I remember, around 70,000 euros per person – and the effect was zero. So now East Germany has the most modern, more than the West, phone system and trains, but the whole social structure is still much less productive.

And another problem is that there was no shared cultural project. For example, do you know a North Korean film, which they tried to show abroad? It is a famous film, *Pulgasari*, directed by Kim Jong-Il. It is about a big monster who helps the people but then demands victims, and the most beautiful girl sacrifices herself for the people, to be eaten. Well, it was even available for a while in the United States, with a small distributor. It was perhaps Kim's biggest attempt. I even have a book published in English by Kim Jong-Il – *On the Art of the Cinema* – and it's wonderful because it mixes political phrases with total platitudes. I love this.

I also saw recently a North Korean film, *The Schoolgirl's Diary*, which was released in France at the end of 2007. It's about a teenage girl who is always sad because her father is away traveling all the time for the devotion to his country. But then her father comes home and explains to her that Kim Jong-Il, the general, is also a human like us – and then the father died at the end of the film. And this teenage girl is so glad and says to the father: "Now I know that you are not here, but I didn't lose a father, I gained another father. Now I have two fathers, you and Kim Jong-Il." It's crazy. If you look at university locations or apartments in the movie, you would have thought that it was an upper-middle-class standard for everyone. In the 1990s, at least 10 percent of the people died from hunger. How did they manage it without any serious rebellions? I know that they are extremely brutal and totalitarian.

My leftist friend, a Chinese philosopher, showed me a photocopy of a textbook for an elementary school in North Korea. They are taught that their leader Kim Jong-Il is so clean that he doesn't shit or urinate. They don't explain how, but he just doesn't. This phenomenon always bothers me. Of course they don't believe it, but nonetheless, on some deeper strange level, they take them seriously. This is my big obsession: people don't mean all these things, yet nonetheless they are crucial.

Let me give you an example. If a rich friend invites you to a restaurant, when the bill comes, of course, it's polite for you to say, "No, please, I will pay. Or let us split." But you both know that you just have to insist a little bit to be polite, and what's so interesting is that we both know this is a game. The most elementary level of symbolic exchange is a so-called "empty gesture," an offer made or meant to be rejected. It is not hypocrisy; it works in some way. Then there are rules and meanings I am aware of, but have to act on the outside as if I am not aware of them – dirty or obscene innuendos which one passes over in silence in order to maintain the proper appearances.

Isn't there a beautiful young ballet dancer in North Korea? But why does North Korea allow this? Do they take her money? What is her status? Somehow they don't criticize her as a traitor but, rather, they use her as a symbol of brotherhood. This also fascinates me.

Is it true that, on the southern side of the demilitarized zone (DMZ) in Korea, there is a unique visitor's site, which can be seen from South Korea, with a theater building with a large screen-like window in front? In front of this theater has been built a completely fake model village with beautiful houses and nicely painted walls, and the people there are even give better clothes to wear, and, in the evening, the lights in all the houses are turned on at the same time – although nobody lives in them – and people are obliged to take a walk. I love this idea. It's like Disneyland. Is this not a pure case of the symbolic efficiency of the frame as such?

Maybe the more they open the cities to show – this is my funny idea – the more North Korea will develop. Why don't they open a platform on Pyongyang which can be looked at from the South? This is the moment of truth: North Korea *behind a mask*. Western observers even think that although North Koreans may be crazy, they're immensely proud and independent. No, they're not. They depend so terribly on what others think about them. But why do they have this obsession to impress others?

In this sense, North Korea fascinates me. How does a society like this actually function? Contrary to what people say, it is a brutal regime. At the same time, it is fragile in the sense that appearances have to be maintained at any price. This already started under Stalinism. If you publish one critical text, or show a moment of weakness to the leader – for example, show Kim Jong-Il sleeping – this is a catastrophe. This is for me the big enigma of communism. It's not just pure brutality but, at the same time, it's an obsession with "feigning" simply to maintain *appearances*. This is a paradoxical point of the ambiguity of politeness that there is an unmistakable dimension of humiliating brutality in the politeness.

This is why, when we had dissidents here, we were all obsessed with thinking that the secret police was watching and listening to us. But I told them that the right model – it's a very racist example – should be this one: I read in some novel by James Baldwin that in the prostitution houses of the old South, of New Orleans before the Civil War, the African-American, the black servant, was not perceived as a person, so that, for example, two white people – the prostitute and her client – were not at all disturbed when a servant entered the room to deliver drinks. They were not embarrassed and they simply went on copulating, since the servant's gaze did not count as the gaze of another person.

The secret police should be treated as black servants once were. You shouldn't care if they listen to you. Who cares? They shouldn't count. You shouldn't be afraid of them and you should ignore them – then it will work nicely. We will later learn that the secret police was always obsessed with this non-existent secret or any big plan. It is a big mistake to think that they don't know there are no secrets. They totally miss the point and waste their energy for nothing. And another *secret of the left* is that we defy and confuse the enemy not by hiding something, but precisely by *not hiding anything*.

13
Deadlock of Totalitarian Communism

You once mentioned that one should never forget the extent to which dissident resistance was indebted to the official ideology. And for this precise reason, I quote: "One can claim that today's North Korea is no longer a communist country, not even in the Stalinist sense." Yet most people generally consider North Korea to be a very communist regime. From an ethico-political perspective, how do you understand the general analysis of North Korea?

SŽ: There are obvious things: we all know that North Korea is a total *fiasco* – I just don't like Western scholars uttering platitudes about them. Some leftists like to say that South Korea is not totally innocent either. Yes, that is right, but we already know all this: before the Korean War in 1948, the South was also being provocative.

I read an interesting thing in the book of a Western historian that for many years in the 1950s, until even the mid-'60s, the standard of living of the average person was higher in North Korea. Because they did have success until the mid-'60s, then it gradually broke down.

This is, I think, the *tragedy* of communism – that it reached a certain level of primitive industrialization, but when the moment (postmodernism, digital technology, or whatever we like to call it) that we are now passing arrived, it didn't work anymore. The irony is that traditional Marxist dogma – the means of production change more rapidly than the relations of production – is absolutely the best way to explain *the fall of communism*. You can also see this very nicely in the book on the communist economy of East Germany.

I know a guy who was a dissident and who worked for one of the top Western journals, whose problem was how to adapt to the digital revolution. He told me that their approach was totally wrong. They didn't see the social dimension of the digital revolution: the local interaction. But their idea was the traditional one. They thought they would be able to make centralized planning more efficient with perfect mega computers. You know, even if bureaucrats have a good plan, when it cannot react fast enough, then it doesn't function. It simply didn't work. This is the irony of the failure, literally, of *totalitarian communism* in the twentieth-century sense.

East Germany was also doing relatively well in the 1950s and the early '60s. Mostly, they were working in a ruined country where reconstruction had to happen fast. In the same way, after 1953, North Korea reconstructed, but in a much more efficient totalitarian way. But then after a certain point, it simply doesn't work any more.

What I'd like to do about North Korea is work out how to interpret this in a way that is *not* racist, because a typical European answer would have been: "Ha ha, you Koreans are primitive. Here is my answer." No, I

don't think so. I think that this has to do with the spe-
cificity of the communist way of doing things, which can
make us arrive implicitly at the true dimension. And this
kind of religious dimension has already been seen with
Mao and Stalin.

Also, late communist regimes have a tendency to
become monarchic. It even happened in Europe, with
Nicolae Ceauşescu. Far from being a result of the
radical break occurring now in Eastern Europe, the
obsessive adherence to the national Cause is precisely
what remains the same throughout this process. And
this attachment was all the more exclusive the more
the power structure was "totalitarian." So, why this
unexpected disappointment? Why does authoritarian
nationalism overshadow democratic pluralism? The
leftist thesis was that ethnic tensions were instigated and
manipulated by the ruling party bureaucracy as a means
of legitimizing the party's hold on power. In Romania,
for example, the nationalist obsession, the dream of
Great Romania, the forceful assimilation of Hungarian
and other minorities, created a constant tension which
legitimized Ceauşescu's hold on power

Nonetheless, whatever you say about classical communist regimes, at one point they were honest and
good. They never allowed direct family succession. For
example, what about Stalin's children? Did they have
any power? No. This was an absolute prohibition.
Succession should not be a family matter. Even Mao:
of course they took care of their children, but were they
privileged? They sent their children to study abroad and
gave them the right to travel, but these were just small
corruptions. There was never a question of Mao's son
becoming his successor.

This tendency, I claim, has something to do with how communism reacted to its decay. It happened in Europe. And in a non-communist way, it also happened in all those crazy countries like Uzbekistan or Kazakhstan. You know who became the father of the nation? Heydar Aliyev, who was the chief of the KGB in the Brezhnev years, a total communist apparatchik. He reinvented himself as the father of the nation [Azerbaijan]. He died about a couple of years ago, and now his son is the president, which is total madness. Again, I really don't want to go into this false racist explanation.

The other thing that interests me is the fact that, even with all its problems, South Korea now has a relatively stable democracy and has already become a successful developed country. South Korea is nothing special, I mean, in a good sense. The point is what critical intellectuals like you can make out of this predicament in which we find ourselves.

Again, here, we should not follow the path of Japan or China. Their models are pretty much the same: to combine traditional wisdom with modernity. I think we need more. The soft fascist solution, which for me is the Chinese solution, simply will not work. My hope is that we will find a new model, not just to retain capitalism and have control through some harmonious corporate means, but to confront the deadlock of modernity in a more intelligent way.

14
The Subversive Use of Theory

Under the so-called Bologna Process, the link between the humanities and theoretical thinking has been questioned, and the colonization of the logic of the market and of capitalist values over the educational field is now crucial. How do you see your educational commitment?

SŽ: This may surprise you: I don't have students. I work all the time as a researcher. This is why I'm eternally grateful to communist oppression. When I finished my studies in the early 1970s, it was during the final moments of hardline communism. So they didn't allow me to teach. I was unemployed for five years, then I got a job at a small research institute. I'm still there. Because it is perfect. I don't have any obligations. Well, I teach here and there a little bit, but I hate students more and more. I like universities *without* students, seriously.

Well, this is – as I would put it – a difficult question. Because it's too easy to say, "Don't think about your career and do whatever you want to do." But, my God, the majority of people have to survive. I think what we should offer them is a way to have some kind of career. Still, the problem for me is how to combine a career with a purpose in life. I mean, you can be a researcher or scientist or whatever, but how can you do something *good* there?

What I want to tell you is that I don't want a society where we are divided into a majority, who are just stupid workers looking for career, and then a minority, who play the morally elevated role. I don't know how it is in your country, but here in Slovenia, Germany, France, or England, what is happening now with education – the so-called *Bologna reform of higher education* – is just horrible.

What they really want is simply the *"private use of reason,"* as I call it, following Kant, so that universities basically produce experts who will solve problems – problems, defined by society, of state and corporate business. But, for me, this is not *thinking*. What is "true" thinking? Thinking is not solving problems. The first step in thinking is to ask these sorts of questions: "Is this really a problem?" "Is this the right way to formulate the problem?" "How did we arrive at this?" This is the ability we need in thinking.

Let's look at the problem with the ideas of those in power. You have, for example, a car-burning incident in the suburbs of Paris. So you call up a psychologist and a sociologist who will tell you, according to their analysis, what to do and how to contain it. No! Thinking is much more than that. It is about asking *fundamental* questions. And this is disappearing. They really want to make universities into schools for experts. It's actually already happening – they've even said it openly – and I'm horrified.

A couple of months ago, the [then] Minister of State for Universities and Science in the UK, David Willetts, openly said that, from then on, "the arts, humanities and social sciences" taught in universities should have nothing to do with the state, meaning that it should be a matter between the university and the individual – the citizen – as an agent of the market. It is a total commercialization of higher education. I think this is pretty much a catastrophe. Because just as in more confused times, like today, we don't just need experts. We also need people who will think more radically to arrive at the real root of problems.

So the first thing to fight for, I think, is simply to make people, the experts in certain domains, be aware of not just accepting that there are problems, but of thinking more deeply. It is an attempt to make them *see* more. I think it can be done. I believe this may be the main task for today: to prevent the narrow production of experts. This tendency, as I see it, is just horrible. We need, more than ever, those who, in a general way of thinking, see the problems from a global perspective and even from a philosophical perspective.

Let's look at another example from ecology. When the oil spill in the Gulf of Mexico unfortunately happened in the summer of 2010, people quickly needed experts to deal with the animals and other sea creatures. No, that's not what we need. Indeed, what should be raised here is a much more fundamental question about such problems, problems for all of us which potentially shatter our commons: "What are the risks if we have to keep the oil drill?" "What kind of industry can replace it?"

Therefore, we should not have only these two extremes: on the one hand, people who are conscious of these issues and, on the other, the majority who just follow their careers and are indifferent to these socio-ecological problems. We should build *bridges between the two*. It was a most beautiful moment, for me, when those really important scientists, from Einstein to Oppenheimer, started to raise more general, fundamental questions about the atomic bomb and other such political issues. So, again, I think it is more important than ever that people become aware that much more is at stake, especially with biogenetics and other scientific development, than just technological problems.

15

Embodying a Proletarian Position

The problem being raised when one is to respond to "the private use of reason" is the fact that this cannot be achieved. We all are aware that there should be certain socio-political responses to this, but still the question of "who?" remains. Who is the subject/agent of revolution? Who is going to make the new world possible?

SŽ: I don't think there is only one agent. There will *not* be a new working class, or whatever. I think they are the people who find themselves in what I call a *proletarian position*: they are sometimes poor, sometimes well-off. What I would like to say about this notion of the proletarian position is that when you are reduced to some kind of zero level, then *another* subject emerges who is no longer the same *self*. I'd like to refer to the book *The New Wounded (Les nouveaux blessés)*, written by the French philosopher Catherine Malabou, who claimed that even now we have a new form of psychic illness. If the twentieth century was defined by hysterical neurosis, now, increasingly, we have a "post-traumatic personality." This is the new order, which means we were submitted to some kind of trauma. It can be rape, public disorder, illness, or whatever. Well, we will survive, but as the living dead, deprived of all our social existence and substance.

When Malabou develops her notion of "destructive plasticity," of the subject who continues to live after its psychic death, she touches the key point: the reflexive reversal of the destruction of form into the form acquired by destruction itself. Quite simply, you are so shocked that, even if you are still alive, yourself, your ego is destroyed. Overdoing it a bit, perhaps, one is tempted to say that the subject deprived of its libidinal substance is the "libidinal proletariat." This is a position of desperation.

In the same way, in ecological terms, we are becoming proletarians. By this I mean that we are deprived of our natural basis. In biogenetics, if it's possible to manipulate even our genetic base, the same things happen.

So my point is that we have to look for *possible proletarian positions*. By proletarian positions, I mean in the sense that we are reduced to the zero level and all objective conditions of our work are taken away from us. This is why I agree with those who claim that the first *Matrix* movie is, in a way, a proletarian film. There is a wonderful scene, which the director didn't exploit further in the movie, where, if you remember, they lie down as if they are dead and the energy is sucked from them. Aren't we, again, reduced to some kind of proletarian position?

Of course, some people are *excluded* – and this is crucial for me. I think what is sad about what we are witnessing now is that Marx was too optimistic. For

Marx, capitalist exploitation has to take place in conditions of legal freedom and equality. That is to say, we all have the same rights formally and legally and we are free, but then, in effect, if you don't have money, you have to sell yourself and you are *exploited*. But now, I claim that worldwide capitalism can no longer sustain or tolerate this *global equality*. It's just too much. I think that, more and more, illegal immigrants or refugees are *in* this problem of what Giorgio Agamben called "*Homo Sacer*." They are in or out, and reduced to a bare existence outside the polis. We are all potentially *homo sacer*, and the only way to avoid actually becoming so is to take preventative measures. This, I think, will be another proletarian position in our time.

And again, look at the proletarian position on the internet. It's clear who will control the internet. What is really worrying, with so-called cloud computing, is a massive *reprivatization* of global spaces. Instead of having big computers with all the data, we will just have our individual machines – PCs, iPhones, etc. – to be connected with limited access; all effective power will be out there. Of course, in a way this is nice. We will have instant access to all the movies, etc. Everything thus becomes accessible, but only when mediated through a company that owns it all: software and hardware, content and computers. The question is, what is this *everything*? Everything will be censored. So cloud computing offers individual users an unprecedented wealth of choice – but isn't this freedom of choice sustained by the initial choice of a provider, in respect to which we have less and less freedom?

To take one obvious example, it's horrendous that Apple made a deal with Rupert Murdoch allowing the news on the Apple cloud to be supplied by Murdoch's media empire. The news you will get from iPhones will be Murdoch's news. This is a problem. The internet interests me as, to use an old-fashioned term, "a field of class struggle." The fight has been going on there from the very beginning. Steve Jobs was no better than Bill Gates. Now I discover Steve Jobs was even worse. Because it's clear how he manipulates it with these machines. It's pure manipulation.

As you may know, the first version of the iPod didn't have a function for phone calls or have a USB connection. It became clear to me, after speaking with someone who is connected with Apple, that he knew the first one would sell well and he wanted people to buy the next generation immediately after. It's pretty horrible. You see that it's not as simple as that. Global access is increasingly grounded in the virtually monopolistic privatization of the cloud which provides this access. The more an individual user is given access to universal public space, the more that space is privatized. I think the key is to prevent these clouds from being privately owned. This is not a technological problem; indeed, it is a purely *ideological* economic decision.

Again, here we have a proletarian problem. In the sense that apparently you have it all, with your iPhone you are connected to everything, but at the same time you have nothing. Everything is outside of you, which means you are somewhat crippled. And now something new is emerging that I cannot but call "private public space." When you chat erotically on the internet, even showing your photos or whatever, you feel like you are in contact with the global world, but you are still isolated in a private space. It's a kind of *global solipsism*.

You are totally alone but in contact with everyone. Or you are in contact with everyone, but, in a way, still not socially connected. Again, interesting things are emerging here.

This would have been my answer. One English analytic Marxist made a very simple but nice point, and I think there is an element of truth in it. He says that, in Marx's time, the proletariat – the good old Marxist determination of the proletarian revolutionary subject – was defined by a series of features: they were from the poorest part of society, the most populated, and they created wealth on behalf of others, etc. Today, we still have all these features, but they are no longer united in *one subject*.

So what I am trying to do is redefine the concept of the proletariat as those who belong to a situation without having a specific "place" in it; they are included but have no part to play in the social edifice. It means that the concept of the proletariat becomes a shifting category. For example, the poorest, these days, are not those who work, but those who are jobless, *excluded*, and so on. So we don't have one subject. We just have to look to see, let's call them, *different proletarian positions*.

And here I have problems with my orthodox leftist friends, who still identify the old notion of proletariat as the working class. To annoy them, I give them this example and it makes them furious. If you stick to the Marxist notion of exploitation and labor theory of value, then you should say that Chávez is exploiting the United States through oil profits. Because Marx, in *Capital*, demonstrates that the natural resources are not a source of value. So this means that we need to rethink the category of exploitation. Marx is absolutely clear here – he even uses oil as an example – that all new value is created by labor. So where do the big profits used to finance the revolution of Chávez come from? From selling the oil and getting money from the United States. So my argument is that we have totally to *rethink* the notion of exploitation and all other features. Everything has to be rethought again.

16

New Forms of Apartheid

*If we are all potentially Homo Sacer, in the sense that
the Marxist notion of the agent is no longer appropriate
for this globalized era, how can the selection of who is
included and who excluded be done ethically? Some must
be excluded as agents of revolution – the notion of fundamental exclusion. Is there a contradiction between your
seeking an ethical, self-critical subject/agent (the barred
subject) of revolution, and your ideas of perpetual revolution? To make a revolution, we need a powerful agent,
but at the same time that agent has to be able to renounce
his power. (The revolutionary state should both use and
renounce power at the same time.) What if you were considered to be among the excluded, and threatened with
death by the revolutionaries?*

SŽ: One thing that still works from the idea of Marx
is that, with capitalism, there exists this radical *gap*. On
the one hand, we have reality, real people working and
consuming, and, on the other, we have this virtual circulation of capital, which goes on and on. There is a gap

between the two. The whole country can effectively be in ruin and people starving, and then a financial expert comes and tells you the economy is in a good state.

We saw just this after the 2008 crisis. The shock was that nothing happened in reality, but all of a sudden we realized that we were in a terrible crisis. I think the problem will be that the crisis will become much more metaphysical and *economically spiritual*. There will be no catastrophe and everything will go on as normal, then, all of a sudden, we will learn that it's catastrophic and everything is wrong. This gap between financial circulation, which follows its own speculative rules, and reality is growing rapidly. I think where we are now is extremely dangerous. I think we are moving toward a much more authoritarian *global apartheid society*.

There are multiple levels. I even tried to enumerate them. I see this problem of *exclusion*, which is no longer about the old class division between workers and capitalists, but simply about not allowing some people to participate in *public life*. They are considered as the invisible ones. In a way, we are all excluded, from nature as well as from our symbolic substance.

So we might say that new forms of *apartheid* are appearing. When we read the book *Planet of Slums*, written by Mike Davis, it's shocking to learn that more than one billion people already live in slums. Slums are exploding, even in China. So we have those who are "*part of no-part*," the "supernumerary" element of society, in slums, which is a very interesting phenomenon because, contrary to what people say, that we live in a society of total control, there are larger and larger populations outside the control of the state. It is as if states allow large parts of their state territory to become off limits. I see a tremendous problem here.

If you go to Los Angeles, everybody knows where the slums are. They are, of course, around the airport. You have huge slums in Inglewood. Do you know why they are there? Because no one cares if there's a lot of noise where only poor people live, so they built the airport there. LA International Airport is located in a perfect place: not far from the airport to the north, for example, is Beverly Hills, which is the richest part of the city. But at the same time, it's a slum area.

In addition to this slum situation, there are other big problems, which I think are economically insolvable. One of them is so-called *intellectual property*. Intellectual products are, in a very naive sense, *communist* by nature. Everybody knows this. Take a bottle of water, for example: when I drink it, then you will not drink it – and vice versa. When we use it, it loses its utility. But with knowledge, it's exactly the opposite. The more it circulates, the more it grows. It's a totally different logic. The difficult task for companies is how to prevent the free circulation of knowledge. Sometimes they spend more money and time trying to prevent free copying than they do on developing products. This is why what is happening now is totally arbitrary.

So it is clear that what Bill Gates did is one big kidnapping. The problem is the following: with physical products, at least up to a certain level, who owns what? You can see this book. I bought it and it's a material object. But when you talk about intellectual products, which circulate, it's always very arbitrary to say they are private property, especially when you apply patents.

Indian farmers – they explained it to me in India – have discovered that certain agricultural methods and materials, which they have been using for centuries, are now owned by American companies, just because an American company patented them. So this American company wants the Indian farmers to pay for what they've been doing for 2,000 years. The next problem will be that when the biogenetic companies patent genes, we will all discover that parts of ourselves, our genetic components, are already copyrighted, owned by others. In the end, your genes will literally be owned by a certain company. So what is you, which is not owned, is just pure Cartesian *cogito*. This paradox is totally absurd.

In all these domains, I think, we can find proletarian positions. Frankly, I don't see any easy way out. But it's clear that the liberal capitalist way will not work. This became evident after the 2008 crisis. Everybody would agree with it now. It's also clear that, in ecology, old-fashioned state regulation will not work. Communism proved that state communism, the way it was, will not work. If there is something clear, it was that communism was even worse ecologically. It's incredible how much worse communism was in that respect.

These are problems of the commons, the resources we collectively own or share. The commons contains nature, biogenetics, intellectual property. So when intellectual property is appropriated by private property we have a new enclosure of the commons. This has given a new boost to capitalism, but in the long term, it will not work. It's out of control.

17

Intrusion of the Excluded into the Socio-Political Space

Particularly in Latin American countries, there have been various attempts to solve the problem of exclusion. Could we find the possibility of emancipatory politics of some sort there? Will it just end up as a failed Latin American populism?

SŽ: There is another problem here. People often take me to be against democracy. I was in England during the 2005 elections when the Labour Party won. And you know what happened? A week before the elections, there was a big TV talk show on the BBC and people were voting about "who is the most hated person in Britain?" Tony Blair won. But a week later, he won the election. This is a very dangerous sign for me. Obviously there is some strong level of dissatisfaction, which cannot be captured by the electoral system. I'm not against democracy. The point is not to criticize democracy in the sense that we need an authoritarian regime. The key is to ask questions about the representative democracy we have today: is it still able to capture the social discontent or formulate the relevant public demands? Or is it getting more and more sterile? We should search for solutions.

In Latin America, for example, the solution they give is to combine representative democracy (the model of Lula or Morales) with social movements. If we vote, do we really even debate what is needed to make big economic decisions, like world trade agreements or crucial economic agreements like NAFTA in the United States? Nobody votes about that. Specialists give you their opinions in a way you cannot judge. But, somehow, the decision is made by them. What we vote about are mostly stupid cultural matters: immigrants, abortion, and all that stuff. This should worry us. It will create an explosive situation. Even after democratic multiparty elections that have been fairly fought, there can still be an extreme level of dissatisfaction which explodes. It's a big challenge. And it's time to start questioning whether this system is really what we aspire to? And if even the experts often cheat, are they really honest?

Another thing that worries me is the reason why China weathered this financial crisis much more easily than elsewhere. The great danger is that all of a sudden, because of its virtual nature, crisis erupts. What is needed more and more are big radical decisions. In the democracy we have now, it's difficult. You have to go through all the mechanisms. But I read a book on China, which is very critical of China, but which nonetheless admits that, when the fiasco happened in 2008, the banks generally put a limit on borrowing because people were not paying back loans, and it was this that eventually pushed the economy further down. But in China, the communist political power bureau gave an order: "No, you should give people even more credit."

———

And it worked perfectly. It is somehow very sad to discover that authoritarian power is much more efficient in these conditions. It also worries me that capitalism is entering a state in which it can still be formally seen as a democracy, but it's really just a ritual, where an actual authoritarian power will work better.

There was one very good argument for capitalism. Let's be frank. Until now, capitalism has always inextricably generated a demand for democracy. It's true there were, from time to time, episodes of direct dictatorship, but, after a decade or two, democracy again imposed itself – like in South Korea or in Chile after Pinochet. But then, things started to move. But I wonder if this so-called "capitalism with Asian values," a Chinese-Singaporean authoritarian capitalism, is not a new form of capitalism, which is economically even more dynamic. It's productive and it functions even better. But it doesn't generate a long-term demand for democracy. Now, however, the link between democracy and capitalism has been broken.

I really think that this is what should worry us, this big divorce slowly developing between democracy and today's capitalism: the success of Chinese communist-run capitalism is an ominous sign that the marriage between capitalism and democracy is approaching a divorce. And here, I'm not into leftist paranoia saying that this is some kind of dark plot. I think it is economic logic *itself*. How to get out of this problem is a big task. I don't have any easy solutions. I just see the problem and urge everyone to look for the solution.

Some of my friends are enthusiastic about Latin American populism. But I am rather skeptical about it as a right solution. I think Chávez was getting crazy and going down and down. Now it's developing slowly into this typical Latin American populism, with a strong leader who made rather strange, eccentric decisions. And it became embarrassing. Chávez prohibited some songs as being dangerous for the morals of the young. And he forced the public station to play some Catholic melodrama. It's simply losing the edge. He became a total, omnipotent leader. He had talk shows: *Aló Presidente Práctico* and *Aló Presidente Teórico*. He discussed theory with the people. Alas, I don't believe in Latin American populism and I think this will ruin it.

Lula was much more efficient. Here I agree with Negri: Lula is more interesting than Chávez. He succeeded, in an almost wonderful way, in keeping things within a democratic framework. He didn't mess with capitalism too much, so it worked, but at the same time he did create a lot for the poor and middle classes. It's incredible to see how much poverty was abolished. Negri is right. Lula followed one of the formulas: one was a purely party democratic system. But he had a problem with his smaller parties, on which he had to rely, so what did he do? Corruption. He systematically paid the small parties to support his power in Parliament. I also would have done the same – it's dirty, but it works.

But when everybody knew and tried to stop him, he did something that was really genius. He and his government collaborated with various social movements – for example, ecologist, workers, and farmers. So the government is related not only to the parties, but also to participatory movements. And this brought a new dynamic. It is a dialectical relation between government and social movements. The *political axis* was not only rooted in the party structure within the government, but was also in constant dialogue, exchanging pressure and cooperation with these movements. The miracle is that he didn't screw it up. Economically it worked. So maybe in the short term this is one of the possible models. Somehow all these civil society movements should think not just about organizing a big demonstration once a year in Trafalgar square or wherever, but about engaging in a more active cooperation. Maybe this is what can work. I don't have any better formulas here.

18

Rage Capital and Risk-Taking Revolutionary Changes

Does activism arise when people feel secure enough to take political risks? For example 1968, during a time of global economic expansion. Or does it take place when people are in severe pain or the rage capital is high enough? What accounts for today's relative passivity in many industrialized countries: too little security and contentedness, or too much?

SŽ: This is a very good question. But I'm still a pessimist. One thing that I don't believe is the simple causality whereby people living in a really bad situation end up by exploding. No, I think it's much more complicated. If you look at all successful revolutions, they usually happen when power is already weakening. Let's take a great anti-communist uprising that occurred in 1956 in Hungary. When Imre Nagy was prime minister, liberalization was already taking place. Also, look at the French Revolution. The king was already losing power by 1785 and they overthrew him when they started to perceive his position as unjustified. Here the shift was purely *ideological*. Revolutions sometimes do happen, maybe in times of chaos. But they usually happen when there's neither a war nor chaos. Revolutions happen under two conditions: in times of poverty, and when justice breaks down. Yet the two are not necessarily connected. Usually in order to realize that your situation is unjust, you must at least experience a certain *ideological freedom*. Because the first step toward freedom is to become aware of your situation – the situation of injustice and unfairness.

Let's look at how feminism started. The feminist movement began not with an attempt to liberate women but with women becoming aware that what they traditionally experienced as a normal situation – being limited to the family and serving their husbands – was not a natural hierarchy but rather a violation of justice. So under what conditions does the revolution occur? The first step in liberation is that you perceive that your situation is unjust. This already is the inner freedom.

This is how we approach the revolutionary situation – as in Egypt now. We have, as you know, all these ideologies of development, globalization, and so on. In the case of globalization, it is very dangerous in a way for capitalism. Imagine an Indian farmer. When he was starving there, totally isolated, why should he rebel? Now he is in contact with the world, seeing what is happening around the world, and he knows what economic development looks like. Not only this, but the official ideology of development – saying that we all should have an equal opportunity – creates expectations. Even in Egypt, if you look at it closely, the correct analysis wasn't that Mubarak was an absolute dictator. I spoke with some people there and learned that there was a small group of people who were allowed to criticize the regime a little bit, and some were not.

So, again, with regard to safety, I think, in order to articulate your rage, you should feel *minimally safe*. Because, if you don't have a feeling of minimal safety, you will not risk showing your rage. This is the way I see the strategy, which was very dirty, that the Mubarak regime took a few days before the revolution. They basically withdrew the police and stopped the trains, because they wanted to create a totally insecure environment – but of course it didn't work, because people showed enough solidarity.

And it's a very typical process that all enemies of democracy, like the conservatives in the United States, focus on. They often say that Egypt is approaching chaos. But, here, things are much more paradoxical. Revolutionary changes don't happen when things are at their worst. Take North Korea, for example. What they need is a minimal openness; people becoming aware of their situation and then the government starting to compromise a little bit. This is why they know they have to remain isolated. Here I also agree with those American liberals who claim that Reagan and Bush were the idiots who kept Castro in power. I entirely believe the statements of liberals who claim that when the United States was saying "You all go to Cuba, it's a wonderful country," hundreds of thousands of Americans, out of curiosity, went to Cuba, so then either Castro would have had to stop this, or it would have all exploded. So this is why, as Herbert Marcuse of the Frankfurt School once put it very nicely in his essay on liberation, "freedom is the condition of liberation." In order to liberate yourself, you must be free. Even in revolution, it goes the same way.

19
Café Revolution

*If we could presuppose the minimal safety and freedom,
what should the leftist revolution aim for?*

SŽ: Again, this is a very good question. I think that we
leftists shouldn't simply believe in chaos. We shouldn't
say – you know, all this horrible leftist strategy –
"the worse it is or the more chaotic it is, the better it
is." The problem is that when the situation is totally
desperate, especially in a situation where you don't
have to organize opposition, it's much more probable
that some dictator or new authoritarian figure will
emerge.

You probably didn't experience the war, but I did. I
can tell you that it's not nice at all to live in that kind of
situation. It's nice to go on a demonstration and then go
and sit in a cafeteria and discuss the demonstration and
so on. To see the public order disintegrate is not a nice
thing. This is why I think that, if you want revolution,
you should be a part of *law and order*. There's nothing
dishonorable about people wanting basic security. My

god, I like to feel safe. Horrible things happen if you don't have this basic law and order.

So again, I claim, things are not as dangerous as we may think. And people believe that the police are usually much more efficient and aligned in authoritarian countries. But this is the myth of strong authoritarian countries. "OK, you don't have freedom, but at least there's order and the police provide security." No, it's not like that! This is why I like to read the history books about everyday life under Stalinism. Beneath the surface, it was extremely violent and chaotic. When somebody beat you, you couldn't do anything. This is a paradox. If you were raped, for example, under Stalinism, and you went to the police station, you know what they would tell you? "Sorry, we cannot take your case. Because we have to report that there is less and less crime in the statistics. If we take cases like yours, it would ruin our statistics." They were simply corrupted.

I never much liked the 1960s, but when I spoke with my friends in France, they used to say that the most beautiful moment in May '68 was when you came in a car from the suburbs, parked it to the north of Notre Dame Cathedral, and walked across the river; then you demonstrated, sometimes burning some cars, but not caring because it's not your car, and then, in the evening, you went north and sat in the café, and debated over coffee. Doesn't this sound interesting?

If there is a lesson from so-called postmodern, post-'68 capitalism, it's that the regulatory role of the state is getting stronger. This was the point of my fight with Simon Critchley. I think it's too easy to say that state power is corrupted, so let's withdraw into this role of ethical critic of power, etc.

But here I'm almost a conservative Hegelian. How many things have to function in order for something to be done? Laws, manners, rules: these are what make us feel truly free. I don't think that people are aware of this fact. That was the hypocrisy of many leftists there: their target was the whole structure of the state apparatus of power. But we still need to count on all the state apparatus functioning.

So my vision is not some utopian community *without* a state. We can call it the state or whatever, but more than ever what we actually need are certain organisms of social power and its distribution. Today's world is so complex. If you want to build a company today, you have to be very deeply entwined with the state apparatus – more and more so. This is why I was always deeply distrustful of those libertarian socialists who claim: "We just want local communal organization." I don't believe in that. I always try to enumerate how many things have to *function* at a state level so that they could do their so-called "local self-management or communal organization."

I think that the left should drop this model of immediate transparent democracy. It cannot be globalized in order to *function*. It needs a very strong state apparatus, which regulates things. If not, things will happen, as you can see today, just like capitalism which is getting so chaotic, especially in the third world.

What fascinates me, therefore, is the idea that we the left should now take over this ideology: "We are the true *law and order*. We are the *true morality*." I very much like this idea of the left taking this position. And my position is that we have to engage wherever we can and do whatever is possible. And all this is what I think we miss in today's left.

20

To Begin From the Beginning

What does it mean to be the moral majority and to represent law and order? What then is today's left missing? What will be the moral obligation of the left today?

SŽ: Well, concerning civility or public morality, you can now see what's happening in art. For any art exhibition in London, for example, to be effective, it must do something disgusting: show some dead fish or the excrement of cows. At one exhibition, my god, they showed a video of a colonoscopy. Today, more and more, the cultural-economic apparatus itself has to incite stronger and more shocking effects and products. These are the recent trends in arts. But the thing is that transgressive excess is losing its shock value. I don't think these transgressive things shock people any more. They have become, to such an extent, part of the system – the operation of today's capitalism. The apparent radicality of some postmodern trends should not deceive us here. So the transgressive model should no longer be our model.

There was a famous scandal in New York almost 10 years ago – a notorious scandal concerning the exhibition "Andres Serrano: Works 1983–93" at the New Museum of Contemporary Art. Many people find his work "Piss Christ," which depicts a crucifix immersed in urine, subversive. But why is this subversive? No! I tried to oppose him. Then he told me that, in this way, he could undermine our standard notion of decency. But I told him "OK, but what's the point? I can film myself shitting in a disgusting way. Then people would say this is subversive. Mr. Žižek started to problematize the notion of disgust!" But why should I problematize this? Some things are simply disgusting. I don't think this is a bourgeois plot or the proletarian reappropriation of high culture, or whatever.

Again, maybe this is one of the solutions that I'm playing with: the left *should* get rid of this idea of saying that we must be subversive and go beyond *good and evil*. No! We have to take over some motives of the so-called *moral majority*. I think the greatest triumph of the ruling ideology has been to keep this moral majority on their side and to present the left as crazy people who think only about having sex with animals and all this dirty stuff. I think, really, the left hasn't yet reached the zero level of crisis.

Here I agree with my friend Alain Badiou, who once said: "*We must begin again*," quoting Lenin from his short text, "On Ascending a High Mountain." Lenin's conclusion – "to begin from the beginning over and over again" – makes it clear that we should drop the continuity with the twentieth-century left. It had its glorious moment, but that story is over. This, exactly, is where we are today, after what Badiou called the "obscure disaster" of 1989, the definitive end of the epoch which began with the October Revolution.

Even with Western social democracy, for example: what is wrong with it as long as it works? Let's take Scandinavian countries. We can be critical of them. I know all those stories about Sweden being really racist and collaborating with the Nazis, etc., etc. But, let me be very naive: in the history of humanity, I don't think there have ever been, at any stage, so many people living such a relatively safe and comfortable life. So when Western European social democracy is still successful, what is so bad about this? Nothing. But the point is that, unfortunately, because of economic necessities, this social democratic system is approaching its end. It cannot work in that way.

There is, radically, a new level of capitalism where everything changes. For example, take personal morality. This is my big problem with my old friend Judith Butler. My problem with post-feminists is that, for them, the enemy is still patriarchal identity politics. But, as I tell them all the time, this is no longer the ruling ideology today. The ruling ideology today is basically something like a vague hedonism with a Buddhist touch. "Realize yourself! Experiment! Be satisfied! Do what you want with your life." It's a kind of generalized hedonism. So what Judith Butler is preaching is a subversive model: "No fixed identity. Reconstruct yourself." But this, I claim, is not the ruling ideology today. Conservatives are just a reaction to this. The basic model is this one: there is no longer a fixed identity.

You see what I mean? We really have to *rethink* it all. Everything should be rethought, one should begin from the zero point. The left is not yet aware of what 1990 meant. It was that all models – the communist state model, the social democratic model, also this immediate democracy model – have failed. So, we should really start to *think again*.

21

The Fear of Real Love

What should the left take as a warning from this failure?
What will we learn from this failed revolution?

SŽ: Let me quote Badiou here. I think this might amuse
you. Now, even sex, in the sense of intensively falling in
love, is going out of fashion. What is fashionable now
are one-night-stands, as shown by all these slogans:
"Don't take bonds too seriously. You must creatively
try homosexuality and heterosexuality. Be open. Don't
fix yourself." Alain Badiou drew my attention to something. He found a wonderful French advertisement for
an internet dating site and matrimonial agency, which
promised: "We will enable you to be in love without
falling in love!" It works both in French and English
with the word "fall" which, in French, is "tomber."
The idea of *falling* in love is considered to be something
terrible. Let's admit it. You have a good, normal life.
Everything is perfect. But when you *fall* in love – I mean
in a true meaning of love – you will be shocked. Falling
in love is really just too traumatic. Because your life will

be totally ruined. We are too narcissistic to risk any kind of accidental trip or *fall*. Even into love.

Well, this is such a *narcissistic economy* that you must have a marital agency. It is somehow a nice idea, but nonetheless here we are basically in a way returning to the pre-modern tradition of arranged marriages or dates. Only instead of parents and relatives, it's the agency that takes on this role. You know why? Because we are afraid of exposing ourselves. We do *not* fall in love. Rather, we look out for better characteristics and economic backgrounds. But it's incredible to see how this actually works. And did you notice, in our narcissistic era, how love or fanatical sexual engagements are themselves becoming transgressive?

I am tempted to link this to another example that really worries me. Something weird is going on in Hollywood. It's a small symptom, but I think it's dangerous. Did you know that the James Bond film *Quantum of Solace* – it's relatively leftist as James Bond saves the Morales regime in Bolivia – was the first Bond film where Bond didn't have sex with the Bond Girl? In all the earlier movies, this happened. This was always the standard ending. James Bond equals "sex in the end."

You can say this is only one example of this *asexual* character. Then did you see the Dan Brown horror movie *Angels and Demons*? In the novel, there is sex between Robert Langdon and Vittoria Vetra. But in the film version, there is no sex. It used to be the other way around. Hollywood inserted the sex. What is going on? Then, take one of the worst novels of all time, *Lost Symbol*. No sex at all – there is not even erotic tension there, nothing. I frankly think that, in the West, we are developing into such a narcissistic culture; we want to be cocooned and safe, and even passionate sex, giving yourself to others, is becoming sex without love – sex is good but in moderation, you know. This reminds me of an explanation that I often use. It's somehow comical. The products we buy in the market have had their damaging ingredient removed: coffee without caffeine, alcohol-free beer, cigarettes without nicotine, even sex without sex. I like this paradox. It illustrates nicely what Freud already said about the paradoxes of the pleasure principle. You see, any form of passionate attachment is seen as a threat in our narcissistic, solipsistic, and individualistic culture.

Everyone knows love is the greatest thing, but, at the same time, it is the most horrible thing. Can you imagine yourself living a nice life and meeting with friends and having one-night-stands, but all of sudden, you fall passionately in love? It's horrible. It ruins your whole life. We are afraid of that. But – how can I put this? – we should *return*, I claim! When Laura Kipnis, an American writer who wrote *Against Love*, said that love is the last form of oppression, I told her: "No! This is today's ideology." Even love, passionate love, is too dangerous.

And it is no wonder that the Catholics are thriving. Because this is the message of the Catholic church: "Don't be too much in love. If you are in love with a girl, marry her. Because then you will see how she is in private, and if you spend all your time together, passion will fade, as usual, and when you need passion you can just go to a prostitute from time to time." My God, you see what a crazy world we live in. There is, on the one hand, more and more obsession with absolute safety, but, at the same time, there is, even within our society, more and more violence in all forms.

This is what I find problematic with so-called *political correctness*. How practically everything you do can be misread. For example, it has actually happened to me in the United States. I looked a woman in the eye and was accused of visual rape. I used a dirty word and was accused of verbal rape. Practically everything you do can be interpreted as aggression. We perceive any excessive proximity of other people to be violence. What fascinates me is how, on the one hand, you have *explosive* forms of *violence*, but at the same time this extremely protective attitude, even, "Just don't come too close to me." I think the discourse of political correctness hides extreme violence. And it is also related to the matter of tolerance. Isn't it interesting that this also fits in with the old Judeo-Christian cliché, the fact that we are afraid of being too close to other people?

I even find this obsession with smoking suspicious. I don't smoke; I am opposed to it, but I find it a little bit suspicious. Did you notice how the same people who are opposed to smoking are often in favor of the legalization of drugs? Why? Because it is fashionable? But wait a minute. Drugs are probably rather more dangerous than cigarettes. All I'm saying is that this campaign against smoking is another sign of the *narcissistic economy*. Especially this obsession with passive smoking, which says: "You smoke? Oh, you are killing me." It is total narcissism. And it is just some crazy theory, which is wrong. What scientists are telling us is that passive smoking can be more dangerous than active smoking. I think today that the discourse of *victimization* is almost the predominant discourse when it says that everyone can be a victim of smoking or sexual harassment. Today we have an extremely narcissistic notion of personality.

So this all adds up, I think, to an absolutely narcissistic economy. We can have sex, but not love, and no passionate attachment, and we need to keep an appropriate distance, and so on. We are really like the Roman Empire in the third–fourth century, when it was in decline. This is a very sad thing. This is why I like to quote the famous lines of a poem by William Butler Yeats, who was right in his diagnosis of the twentieth century. In his poem *The Second Coming*, he wrote: "The blood-dimmed tide is loosed, and everywhere / the ceremony of innocence is drowned; / the best lack all conviction, while the worst / are full of passionate intensity." Is this not a good description of today's split between anemic liberals and impassionate fundamentalists? Where do you find passion today in politics? Even though the so-called Christian or Muslim fundamentalist is a disgrace to true fundamentalism, we can only find this passion with *fundamentalists*. The best are no longer able to fully engage themselves, while the worst engage in racist or religious fanaticism. This is what makes me sad.

22

Dialectic of Liberal Superiority

For another example of passion in political engagement and commitment, unlike the one of fundamentalists, I'm thinking of people like Anna Politkovskaya, a Russian journalist, who was assassinated. She was the one who took enormous risks to uncover the hidden stories of war in Chechnya and who opposed the Russian President, Vladimir Putin. Do you think that courage is contagious? That many can be moved by the courage of Politkovskaya, for example? What role might such contagious courage play in social change, including revolution? Is there a source of some kind of seriousness or guidance – as we might see in Simone Weil or others?

SŽ: First of all, I am against Putin. I don't think that things are as clear as that. Of course it's horrible what they did to Mikhail Khodorkovsky, but he was no angel. You can't become the richest man in Russia by being a humanist. Although I am intrigued by this person. I believe that Khodorkovsky tried to do better because he was probably intelligent, and he got the idea that if you organize it better for workers in the long term, it functions. Even the case of Alexander Litvinenko. It was of course horrible what the Russians did, but he wasn't just a good, honest guy. There were different struggles and scandals on finding radioactivity on a fax machine, and poison, etc. Otherwise, I totally sympathize with Politkovskaya; I think all this has to come out.

But what I don't like is that you often find an aspect of satisfaction in saying: "Oh, poor Russia. But we know . . . ." I always find it suspicious that, when you sympathize with freedom fighters in other countries, the conclusion is usually like this: "Look at those poor guys, but with us everything is okay." If you take Stieg Larsson seriously, you can see strange things are also happening in our own countries.

So you don't even have to take enormous risks like Politkovskaya. From my experience of just a normal academic life – I don't know how it is in Sweden, but I can tell you about the United States and here in Slovenia – there is so much conformism, back-stabbing, and plotting going on. What I'm saying is that if you are worried about honesty and want to fight for something big, don't look for fights out there; you have *enough* fights and struggles here. I, of course, support them, but I just don't like this *liberal superiority*.

I also find this myth that the Putin regime is harsh but effective to be problematic. It is simply not true. He's just the voice of the majority of the oligarchs. His class bases are still oligarchic. As we all know, in the financial crisis, the state used its enormous reserves to help the oligarchs much more than ordinary people who were in trouble.

So, again, I totally reject the Putin propaganda that

says: "OK, he may be a little harsh but that is the only way in Russia to prevent oligarchs from taking power over the people." No! In every crisis, he let the ordinary people suffer to the end. This is why I don't want to visit Russia now. Because I visited Russia six years ago, but then I discovered that those who invited me were people who are close to Putin and they tried to appropriate me. So now I would prefer to visit other groups in Russia and I don't want to be seen there as part of the Putin circle.

It was the same in China when I visited Shanghai. It was a wonderful scandal. I like it. I basically provoked them: my translator there was an old lady. She was an old, dignified lady, and when I started to speak, illustrating the obscenity of ideology, she was so embarrassed that she stopped translating and almost lost consciousness. But she gave me a nice answer. She was nonetheless funny. In the end, I learned that she also translated for Clinton when he visited China on some business trips after his presidential term. So I asked her: "How do you compare Clinton to me?" She gave me a wonderful answer. Everyone laughed and applauded. She said: "You talk a lot about sex, but Clinton does it." It was a wonderful answer.

It was also very funny when a sexually liberated young girl told me how penetration is oppressed, but the girls want to be fucked, want to be penetrated, etc. I told them: "It's very strange. If this were in the United States, you would have been accused of being phallocentric." But nonetheless I am so interested in China because there is a certain degree of *artistic freedom*. It is incredible how many unwritten rules they have about what you *can* say and what you really *cannot* say. I ask them how it was with Mao Zedong. They said with Deng Xiaoping's judgment: "70 percent good, 30 percent bad." Then I told them, "OK, I am allowed to write a book called 30 percent. We know what was good, so now let's talk a little bit about what was bad." They told me: "Of course not. We can't!"

For example, there was the traumatic period in the late 1950s: the Great Leap Forward. How many people died then? Mao caused the greatest famine in history by exporting food in order to buy nuclear weapons. Somewhere between 36 and 38 million people starved and were slave-driven to death at that time. Even worse, the Mao government knew exactly what was going on. This is instrumental attitude at its most radical. It was a mega-tragedy. But people are not allowed to read or talk about this, and it is very interesting that a book about it is prohibited in China but was published in Hong Kong. And whenever they talk about it in public, they are not attacked as being a traitor, but are simply ignored. Nothing happens. This is a typical Chinese solution. I don't like that model.

This is how things are going: you just mention certain things, but you are not allowed to go into details. For them, here is a good formulation of Lacan: the pervert is the instrument of the other's desire. They are precisely the "perverts," I would say. They always have the answers: never the questions, only the answers. They are not a danger but an annoyance. They pretend to have the answers, but totally without anything substantial.

But we need to deal with our heritage. I don't like the left that has the attitude: "Yes, Stalinism was bad. But look at the horrors of colonialism!" Here I am very critical of Adorno and Horkheimer in *Dialectic of Enlightenment*. They are an extreme example. The task is still ahead. With all the horrors of the twentieth century, the liberals' account is insufficient. It remains for the left to explain this.

23
The Day After

Let us talk about hope. You mentioned the revolutionary changes of our time. What action/movement gives you the most hope? Can you see any seedling or example of revolutionary change? Can you give us an example of that?

SŽ: The problem is that hope and *horror* are always intermingled. What is happening in these days in Egypt and other Arab countries is, of course, hopeful. Almost everyone in postmodern times thinks nothing can happen. But it has been so nicely falsified. It did happen: a very traditional uprising without any religious references, but just calling for human dignity and secular demands. It's a wonderful event. And it's a *real event*. What I mean by a "real event" is that it's not just a smooth transition. We are living in this moment of uncertainty and you don't know who is in power, and this, of course, shows that there is hope. Hope simply means *an open moment* when you don't know who is in power, and then the regime falls apart.

But the problem is that, in these situations, there

is hope and, at the same time, there are confusing times where you end up with an even worse regime than before. In Germany, for example, there was hope among the strong leftists in the early 1920s, but then they got Hitler. In Iran, it was the same. People were originally hopeful about the Khomeini revolution. It was also an emancipatory explosion. But after two years of hard internal fighting, all the leftists had been wiped out and today they have Mahmoud Ahmadinejad. Now the struggle is still going on, and this for me is the true hope. For example, do you remember the big demonstration against Ahmadinejad organized by Mir Hossein Mousavi, who should have won the presidential election? This is clear proof that the Islamists didn't really win in Iran. The struggle is still going on, and there is tremendous resistance. My point is that there's still a lot of hope, but hope is always mixed with danger. The situation is so complex. I simply don't see any political movement about which I would say, I'm for it or not.

Take Latin America. It started well, and then it got lost. This makes me sad because what I really care about is not those big enthusiastic moments like now in Egypt. I'm much more of a realist here. What interests me is *the day after*. That is to say: out of this enthusiastic moment that makes us feel free, how will this be translated into a new institutional order? What will this order be? Will it be simply a Western liberal democracy? Or will it be some kind of Islamic fundamentalist regime? Or will it be something *new*? I mean this is a real hope for me: that something will emerge out of these popular revolts that is neither just a corrupt Western democracy – which just means liberal elites who ignore the crowds – nor an Islamist hardline fundamentalist regime. I think this possibility means *real* hope.

But true hope rises from what we can't even learn in the media. I don't know how much it is reported in your country, but, for example, are you aware of what is going on in India? Almost one million Naxalite Maoists there have been mounting major rebellions. Horrible things have been happening back in the jungles of central India. They're discovering new minerals, and are just killing the tribes in an extremely brutal way to make it free to industrialize. The Indian prime minister characterized this rebellion as the "single largest internal security threat," and furthermore, the main media, which present it as extremist resistance to progress, are full of stories about "red terrorism." Nonetheless, as Arundhati Roy wrote in *Outlook India* magazine, the Maoist guerrilla army consists of just poor and desperate tribal people, who have been mercilessly exploited, raped, and cheated by moneylenders, fighting only for survival. Their situation is precisely that of Hegel's rabble: the Naxalite rebels in India are a starving tribal people, to whom the minimum of a dignified life is denied.

Yet India is considered one of the largest democratic countries. People always oppose India to China. China is a totalitarian society, which is bad, and India is the biggest democracy in the world. Did you see that stupid film *Slumdog Millionaire*? You remember the beginning where the small guy, not a thief at all, was accused and they tortured him with electricity? When I was in India, I asked my friends whether it is still done like this. Then they said: "Yes, it is totally normal. Every police station has machinery to torture using an electric shock. And it's done regularly to everyone. They just use it all the time." He told me that, in India, the critics of those in power employ irony: "Please at least treat us like the Chinese treat the Tibetans where they torture you only if they suspected you of having links with the Dalai Lama's politics." They don't torture ordinary small thieves. But, in India, they torture everyone.

So, again, I now see signs of hope there, yet the media ignore them. They are presented only as Maoist or terrorists and so on. But what the army is doing in India is horrible. They treat them like Americans in the nineteenth century treated the Native Indians. It's extreme brutality. They say, "We will civilize the region," but it means that the army rape the women and burn the houses. This is the tragedy today. Yet, hope is always connected with danger, potential chaos.

And this is a tough decision to make. Because it is clear apropos of Egypt. Western liberals, those who are in power, are, I think, too opportunistic. They say "No" to any better choice or any change, because every change is dangerous. I think we have to take a chance. I think precisely because of this attitude – "No changes in Arab countries. It's better to have dictators and tyrants who are friendly to us" – that they will experience stronger and stronger uprisings. This is why I quoted the old motto of Mao Zedong in my article on Egypt, "Why fear the Arab revolutionary spirit?" published in the *Guardian*: "There is great chaos under heaven – the situation is excellent." This is the price you have to pay for the risk. If you say "No" to change, it can be chaos and nothing will change, so the situation will just get more and more explosive.

This again is the danger: to know how to walk this

hazardous narrow path where there is great danger but, at the same time, there is hope. True hope for me only exists where there is danger. Walter Benjamin already said: "Every rise of fascism bears witness to a failed revolution." His old thesis not only still holds today, but is perhaps more pertinent than ever. So history brings situations, which are hopeful and dangerous, and it's up to us what to do.

24

The Universality of Political Miracles

What, then, do you see as a sign of tragedy, rather than of hope? And speaking of a crucial moment in Arab countries, can Egypt's revolt lead to a new political reality?

SŽ: What I find so tragic in Western Europe today is the fact that the only passionate political agent, more or less, is predominantly the right-wing anti-immigrant populist, who brings the voice of popular discontent and change. The only passion is there. This is a very tragic situation. So I'm a pessimist for Europe.

Nonetheless Europe historically presented something nice. For me, moments of hope are always moments of *universality*. Do you know how often we talk about a multicultural culture, where we are suspicious about universalism? People often say that we are just too naive, and we all live in our own cultures, and there is no such thing as universality. But listen! What affected me tremendously, not only looking at the general picture of Tahrir Square but also listening to the interviews of protestors and participants, is how cheap and irrelevant this talk about multiculturalism becomes. There we all were fighting against tyrants; they wanted dignity and freedom and immediately found solidarity with each other. Here we already find universality. We have absolutely no problem identifying with them. That was the wonder of this revolution. And this is how we build universal solidarity. It's a struggle for freedom, and freedom is universal.

I think the greatest triumph is this: when some Muslim brotherhood members were interviewed by the media, they honestly said, first, that this was not their revolution, but they just support it, and, second, that the goal was democracy, freedom, economic justice, and so on. Isn't it nice that even the fundamentalist political agents had to adopt this language – the language of secular demands for democracy?

This is the opposite of Iran. In Iran, the Khomeini revolution is basically more religious. Leftist Marxists had to smuggle themselves in talking an Islamic language. Here is the opposite. In Egypt, Islamics have to talk using a secular language. This is a wonderful event. I mean nobody believed that they could raise Arab crowds on purely secular grounds. Everybody thought: "Oh, maybe some elite liberals have to come. Arabs are too stupid and too conservative so whatever they need is religion." No! they did it. Even if it turns out to be a fiasco, this is hope.

Here I'm tempted to quote Emmanuel Kant's notion of *the sublime*. Kant interpreted the French Revolution as a sign that pointed toward the possibility of freedom. In spite of all the horror that goes on there, events like the French Revolution give you hope – that there's some kind of universal tendency to freedom and progress.

Kant concluded with the fact that, although progress cannot be proven, we can discern signs indicating that progress is possible. This is what an event like this means. One should note here that the French Revolution generated enthusiasm not only in Europe, but also in faraway places like Haiti, where it triggered another world-historical event. The hitherto unthinkable happened: a whole people fearlessly asserted their freedom and equality. I think we should remain faithful to them.

Do these words not also fit perfectly the ongoing Egyptian uprising? The French Revolution was, for Kant, a sign of history in the triple sense of *signum rememorativum, demonstrativum, prognosticum.* The Egyptian uprising is also a sign in which the memory of the long past of authoritarian oppression and the struggle for its abolition reverberates; an event which now demonstrates the possibility of a change; a hope for future achievements. Whatever our doubts, fears, and compromises, in that instant of enthusiasm, each of us was free and participating in the universal freedom of humanity. All the skepticism displayed behind closed doors, even by many worried progressives, was proven wrong. And also we should be realists. But nonetheless, we should be open to a kind of *miracle.* Things like this are miracles. I don't mean in religious terms. I mean miracles in the sense that things like this always explode against the predictions of all the specialists, who are always wrong.

Well, I'm old enough to remember the Khomeini revolution. I remember a British general, Sir John Hackett, wrote a book, *The Third World War: The Untold Story,* three or four years before the Khomeini revolution in 1980, depicting the new world conflict. In Slovenia we all laughed at it. Because the decisive battlefield between East and West was supposed to take place 20 kilometers northeast of Ljubljana. But what's interesting is the presupposition of that book. It says that there will be chaos in the Middle East, and the only American ally that is totally faithful is Iran. You know, it was such a shock for everyone in Iran. Nobody expected it in Iran. They all thought that there could be chaos in Egypt, but not in Iran.

This is exactly what is happening in Tunisia today. Everybody thought there could be chaos here and there, but not in Tunisia – it is the country where tourism is doing well and everything works peacefully. People even described Tunisia as the country, by definition, where nothing happened. But now we have a revolution there. So I think we should be open to this miraculous aspect: again, not a miraculous thing in the sense of God or religion, but a miraculous event in the sense that something can emerge out of nowhere. We cannot predict anything. *Political miracles* give me hope.

25

Messianism, Multitude, and Wishful Thinking

It is obvious that events – political miracles as you call them – are taking place, but who will make these political miracles happen, not in the sense of populist demonstrations or uprisings but, rather, a change of political structure and economic systems? Can the "Multitude," according to Negri and Hardt, be the way forward, or at least an alternative – despite the crucial critiques of the actual possibility of its holding on to political power?

SŽ: No, not the multitude. Negri and Hardt basically use this term almost in a religious sense – I've been having a long philosophical debate with them about this. The problem with multitude is that it mobilizes a certain philosophical topic, such as the difference between presence and representation. The idea of multitude is the presence of absolute democracy and it is always against political representation. And then, the goal is to achieve some kind of immediately transparent democracy. I don't think this works.

I'm not against representation. As Claude Lefort

and others have amply demonstrated, democracy is never simply representative in the sense of adequately representing (expressing) a pre-existing set of interests, opinions, etc., since these interests and opinions are constituted only through such representation. Yet global capitalism today can no longer be combined with democratic representation. Hardt and Negri aim at providing a solution to this predicament in *Empire*, as well as its follow-up, *Multitude*. I don't think this *dream* of getting rid of all forms of representation and arriving at some kind of immediate transparency, so called "absolute democracy" – "the rule of everyone by everyone, a democracy without qualifiers, without ifs or buts" – will work. I think Negri and Hardt's intention is to repeat Marx.

All I can tell you is that the Marxist dream of there being *one* big agent of social change is illusory, just like the traditional Marxist answer to those who fought for the rights of women, ecology, or racism. Can't you see that all these depend on capitalism? I still think that *capitalism* is the key problem. But nonetheless I don't think that we have one agent, as it was historically predestined to be. As Hegel already knew, "absolute democracy" could only actualize itself in the guise of its "oppositional determination," as terror. So this kind of mirror image of a reliance on Marx is their political deadlock. So, when Naomi Klein writes, "Decentralizing power doesn't mean abandoning strong national and international standards – and stable, equitable funding – for health care, education, affordable housing and environmental protection. But it does mean that the mantra of the left needs to change from 'increase funding' to 'empower the grassroots'," one should ask the naive question: *How?* How are these strong standards and funding – in short, the main ingredients of the welfare state – to be maintained? What would "multitude in power" (not only as resistance) be? How would it function?

Again, the agents of change are, as I describe them, somewhat related to my idea of different *proletarian positions*. It means those people who are deprived of their substance, like ecological victims, psychological victims, and, especially, excluded victims of racism, and so on. It is effectively surprising how many features of slum-dwellers fit the good old Marxist determination of the proletarian revolutionary subject: they are "free" in the double meaning of the word even more than the classic proletariat ("freed" from all substantial ties, dwelling in a free space, outside the police regulations of the state); and they are a large collective, forcibly thrown together, "thrown" into a situation where they have to invent some mode of being together, and simultaneously deprived of any support in traditional ways of life, in inherited religious or ethnic life-forms.

26
Politicization of Favelas

Speaking of proletarian positions, added to the failure of multitude as an agent for change, it is not easy to capture the image of this term. An instant reactive image to this ambiguity might be slum-dwellers. How would you illustrate it? How do you think this abstract notion could involve the revolutionary potential? Or, as you once put it, was it a purely contingent drift, something which simply emerged "because, among all these possibilities, there was the possibility to emerge" (as Varela put it), or can we risk a more precise evolutionary account of its prehistory?

SŽ: My big hope is what happens in *slums*. I spoke with my Brazilian friends who told me how the government is playing dirty at this point. Of course what predominates in slums is an inner mafia – gangsters or religious sects, etc. But, from time to time, various kinds of new social rebel, less progressive, start to organize themselves. At least in Brazil, do you know what, as they told me, always happens at that point? All of a sudden drugs become available. The police consciously allow drug-related crime, and this criminal activity puts political awareness on the back burner. It's a very dirty game. After every political mobilization in the slums, drugs are available. But it's those in power who do it.

Do you remember the *coup d'état* against Solidarność in Poland? And again in Poland, after Wojciech Jaruzelski's *coup d'état* in 1980? All of a sudden, drugs were readily available, together with pornography, alcohol, and Eastern Wisdom manuals, in order to ruin the self-organized civil society. My friends from Poland told me it wasn't just communist repression. After the *coup*, communists allowed something very primitive but effective to happen. Of course they oppressed political activity, but at the same time it was very easy to get hold of drugs and pornography. They even supported Buddhist transcendental meditation. All this was just to distract younger generations from political activity. Religion, drugs, and sex are good just to depoliticize.

This is why Badiou is right in denying to the enthusiastic events of the collapse of the communist regimes the status of an Event. This way, one can continue to dream that revolution is round the corner: all we need is authentic leadership, which would be able to organize the workers' revolutionary potentials. If one is to believe them, Solidarność was originally a worker's democratic socialist movement, later "betrayed" by its leadership, which was corrupted by the Church and the CIA. There is, of course, an element of truth in this approach: the ultimate irony of the disintegration of communism was that the leaders revolt.

So maybe there is potential in the slums. Mike Davis may well be correct when he argues that "there's a consensus, both on the left and the right, that it's the slum peripheries of poor Third World cities that have become a decisive geopolitical space." This would be, for me, a true miracle: *politicization of the slums.* You know why? Slums are interesting because people are thrown into them without any regard to ethnic division or given unity. People there are usually from mixed levels of life. Also the only way to unite them would have been a more political one and I think this is why I still have some sympathy for Hugo Chávez. In spite of all the stupid things he did, he was the first one who really included people from slums, like *favelas*, in political-social life.

Even in Brazil they want other countries to help them in a humanitarian way, but this isn't humanitarian help, because one doesn't politically mobilize them. I'm not talking here as a naive revolutionary, but rather as a kind of conservative, because, I claim, if we don't do this, then we come closer and closer to a kind of *permanent emergency state*, where parts of society in the slums will be invisible and there will be a kind of low-level civil war.

Like in France where, you remember, there were car-burning rebels in Paris about three years ago. This I think is a model of today's form of revolt: a bad one. It was a very mysterious thing. It wasn't some conservative Islamist movement, and it didn't have any ideology. The first thing young people in the suburbs burned were their own mosques and cultural centers. It was a kind of pure protest *without a program*. It was, quoting Roman Jakobson in linguistics, the notion of "phatic communication." The goal is not to pass information but just to signal, "Hi, I'm here." The point is just to tell you this. There was no positive message of wanting more justice or dignity. It was a big explosion of violence. But the message was, basically, "Hi, we are here." It is a danger-ous situation when young people just have this *abstract discontent.*

Bernard-Henri Lévy, a guy whom I don't like much, told me that Sarkozy, at that time Interior Minister, sent not only police but also social workers to the site, and he even organized Muslim priests to go to these young people and ask them "What do you want?" And they didn't get an answer – they didn't express any demands, just an abstract discontent and pure explosion. Isn't this a set sign of Western European societies? That you get this kind of pure explosion of violence, which cannot even formulate a minimal utopian program. Here, again, this is a dangerous moment.

So the principal task of the twenty-first century is to politicize and discipline – the "destructured masses" of slum-dwellers. Today's historical situation does not compel us to drop the notion of the proletariat, of the proletarian position; on the contrary, it compels us to radicalize it to an existential level well beyond Marx's imagination. We need a more radical notion of the proletarian subject, a subject reduced to the evanescent point of the Cartesian *cogito*, deprived of its substantial content. For this reason, the new emancipatory politics will no longer be the act of a particular social agent, but an explosive combination of different agents. The ethico-political challenge is to recognize ourselves in this figure – in a way, we are all excluded, from nature as well as from our symbolic substance. Today, we are all potentially a *Homo Sacer*, and the only way to stop actually becoming one is to act preventively.

So what we find in "really existing slums" is, of course, a mixture of improvised modes of social life, from religious "fundamentalist" groups held together by a charismatic leader and criminal gangs up to seeds of a new "socialist" solidarity. The slum-dwellers are the counter-class to the other newly emerging class, the so-called "symbolic class" (managers, journalists, and PR people, academics, artists, etc.). What we should be looking for are signs of new forms of social awareness that will emerge from the slum collectives: they will be the seeds of the future.

27

Bolivarianism, the Populist Temptation

You mentioned Chávez and slums of favelas *famous for having the highest crime rates in the world. What went wrong there? The "Bolivarian Revolution" seemed so promising, with Chávez's participatory ideas concerning oil money and the slums, but they ended up with such negative consequences.*

SŽ: I don't know the exact causes. But although Chávez wanted people to participate, the problem was the way local self-organization was connected to the state. Why? It became brutally hard to get money and help from the state. It wasn't purely local self-organization; it was self-organization subordinated to the state in order to get money. And because of this, of course, it exploded into corruption, into inefficiency, etc. It just showed us that when we combine local self-organization and the state, it becomes authoritarian, and you can end up with a dangerous mix of *populist violence*.

Another dangerous game is the following one: Chávez

tries to ignore the problem of violence. I heard they somehow prohibited the reporting of revolts in the media because a much darker thing is happening there. This is what my leftist friends told me: Chávez thought that those who are horrified by violence are mostly from the middle classes. The idea is that poor people are exerting more violence against the middle classes. But since Chávez considered the middle classes to be his enemies, his idea was this: "Fuck them. Let's have a little bit of violence!" He played a very dangerous game here.

Chávez is lost steam. It is a real tragedy. Because he played these populist games, he neglected the physical infrastructure. The machinery of oil extraction is falling apart, and they are compelled to pump less and less. Chávez started well in politicizing and mobilizing the excluded, but then he fell into the traditional populist trap. Oil money was a curse for Chávez, because it gave him space to maneuver rather than confront the problems. But then he had now he must confront them. He had enough money to patch things up without solving problems. For instance, Venezuela has experienced a massive brain-drain to Colombia and other places: it is, in the long term, a catastrophe. I am distrustful of all these traditions, "Bolivarianism," etc. – it's all bullshit.

I have a very leftist friend who told me how this really looks. He told me he was in a middle-class restaurant with friends in the center of Caracas. Three or four of Chávez's fanatic guards came in and started to shout and laugh at a woman. Nobody said anything. They were totally intimidated, in a state of constant terror. You know, I'm saying something very bourgeois, not Marxist, but it's true that Lenin was aware of this: you need an effective middle class that can organize production and societal development. Without this, you can do nothing good. What Chávez was doing is horrible.

All revolutions have this kind of *original sin*. For example, in Cuba, do you know what one of Castro's sins was? In 1958, when Castro was already holding the eastern part of the island of Cuba and had made the final pushes to get Havana, he knew that the main object was to get the elite behind him. The purely Spanish, not mestizos, not mixed: the intellectuals, doctors, and so on. And he played the racism card more or less openly. Remember that the dictator whom Castro overthrew was Batista, who is a half black mestizo. And Castro's propagandists spread rumors to all those elite loyal Hispanics: "Allow us to take power and black slaves will no longer rule you." It's true now if you look at the structure of the Cuban elites; of course there are a couple of symbolic impotent black figures. But when you turn on the TV, count the faces, and look at how many blacks you see there. We can see that a pure Hispanic elite rules that society. You can see a couple of women to fill the quota, making it appear better, and there are some ministerial posts occupied by women, but they are the ones that a macho society typically gives to women, like healthcare or education. These are for women and, in practice, for blacks. Remember, you would never have guessed that in Cuba pure Hispanics are in the minority; the majority consists of mestizos and then pure blacks.

Incidentally, in Brazil it's the same. Look at all the elite there. Even leftists around Lula, they are all white. You would never have guessed that black people make up over 40 percent of the population in Brazil. And typically, in Lula's government, there was one black guy, and he was a minister of culture, a silly post. He was put there for the sake of appearances, and was allowed just to organize his concerts and propaganda and whatever. They don't allow him to have any real power. Unfortunately, one has to pay the *price* for a political choice.

28

Violent Civil Disobedience

As you mentioned the car-burning rebels in Paris, the leftist revolutionary gesture is someway typically stigmatized as a violent one. So the problem of violence in the process of revolution must be critical, especially in your context. How do you understand, within this framework, the violence of the French banlieues? What is your definition of violence? What, today, is the relation between violence and politics? Can any violence be justified for any reason?

SŽ: What I'd like to insist on in this case is that, like in Egypt, an actual revolution takes place, as you could see, in a pure way. The only violence there was *symbolic violence*. Symbolic violence in the sense that you walk in the street and ignore the authorities. Demonstrators didn't kill anyone. Violence always occurs after the authorities step in. Even if you look at the French Revolution, it was the same. Forget about all those stories you know about terrorism or violence. Every good historian will tell you that before and after the Jacobins in the French Revolution there were many more people killed. But they were insignificant and ordinary people – nobody cares about them. When you kill some well-known prince, then everyone talks about it as terror.

I think the logic is this. First, there's invisible violence going on all the time. We must be very careful when we talk about violence. I quoted in my book, *Living in the End Times*, a wonderful sentence from Mark Twain's *A Connecticut Yankee in King Arthur's Court*: "A city cemetery could contain the coffins filled by that brief Terror which we have all been so diligently taught to shiver at and mourn over; but all France could hardly contain the coffins filled by that older and real Terror, that unspeakably bitter and awful Terror, which none of us has been taught to see in its vastness or pity as it deserves." You know, it's ridiculous. In order to grasp this parallax nature of violence, one should focus on the short circuits between different levels, between, say, power and social violence, yet it should be experienced as *violence*.

For example, in Egypt, if 100 people die, it's horrible. But are you aware of how many people die regularly of torture and terror even at times when there is *nothing particular going on*? For me, the big question, when you talk about violence, is always what goes on in apparently normal times. At times like this, people perceive the situation as peaceful. Are we really *aware* of how much violence happens during these periods? I don't mean some sort of poetic violence. By violence, I mean extremely brutal violence: torturing, starving, beating, and whatever. It went on all the time in Egypt: their prisons were so terrifying, horrific. So again, that's my first point.

My second point is that this is the logic of authentic revolution. People are violent when they raise a revolution. Of course, there may always be excesses. But as you can see here clearly, they are extremely marginal. Most people are violent just in the sense of ignoring power. When the policeman tells you: "You shouldn't go there," you say "Fuck you. No! I will go there." Remember those magic moments when the authorities allowed people to gather in Tahrir Square. Violence stopped. People were there just demonstrating.

Violence comes, as a rule, from the other side. It comes from those in power who think that they have to scare people to create violence. It's not that I advocate violence in the sense of, "Oh, let's do some killing." I'm just saying that the move people should make, of course, is a kind of massive boycott-style of violence, which is totally non-violent in the sense of there being no killing or torturing people. The problem is what happens when the other side starts to counter-attack. Even then, as a revolutionary, you usually don't have the wherewithal to make a counter-attack, but you must somehow resist and defend yourself. Here I agree with Badiou. The left should learn, from the twentieth century, the horror of state terror or violence. Violence of leftist progressives should basically be *defensive violence*, in the sense that "We occupy the square. We defend if you attack us – but not this kind of aggressive violence."

Like now, wonders can be done here. I think that just ignoring the crowds was masterful. Remember when the army tanks started to arrive? Instead of attacking them, they started to embrace them, even treating them as friends. It was masterful because it was a very reasonable way to behave, even if the army wasn't as good as the government claimed or even if they sent hundreds of tanks. It was clear that the army would have been going too far if they had simply started to shoot at the people. So why not simply receive them? What does it mean? Nothing. Even though there were some tanks, people ignored them and went on to embrace the soldiers. Isn't this a model of how to resist?

And even if you take a violent act to be a problem, take Wikileaks. People claim it is violent in the sense that it can cause catastrophes. But didn't Wikileaks do it in a very moderate way? Some people think it was too moderate. From what I know, they didn't just publish everything. They only gave certain information to four or five big media outlets, for example, some names of the spy in China who may then be arrested or killed. Yet still, didn't they do it in a moderate and considerate way? I think it should be acceptable.

The only violence that I advocate is in situations where there is a terrorist or autocratic violent regime – usually you might call it, although it's maybe a little more radical, *civil disobedience*. Like when you start to behave as if you don't admit the legitimacy of public authority. And then you create your *free territory* in this way. Violence should only be defensive. I don't find anything problematic about this.

29
Legitimacy of Symbolic Violence

So you mean that the defensive form of violence is legitimate? But can it be revolutionary enough to make actual changes? Isn't that just too naive a concept of the violent act?

SŽ: Although it is in a different context, let me tell you a funny story. When the Kurdish resistance in Turkey was much more active, I could not but sympathize with them. I was told by my leftist friend in Eastern Turkey that conditions in prisons about 15–20 years ago were horrible. People were tortured, suspected of being combatants. Then they did something to the guardians, after which nobody was killed. My god, I find it too strange that this was acceptable. They discovered that the guardians who did the torturing were from the local area. So Kurdish people from outside discreetly approached one of the guardians after office hours and said: "We know you're torturing our people to death. But we know who you are and where you live. If you go on torturing, we will kill your wife and children." All of a sudden, the torture stopped. Isn't it funny? Conditions in prison started to get better and the guards treated the prisoners decently. I'm sorry, but this was a desperate measure, I would say a scam.

But can you imagine a truly horrible situation? Can you imagine someone who is very close to you being held somewhere and raped and tortured and you know all about it but *cannot do anything*? I cannot even imagine my son or a woman I love dying suddenly as a result of some kind of an explosion and never hearing about it. But it could happen. This is, for me, the worst thing. And under those conditions, you have to fight back. It's not enough to protest. To call foreign journalists and to do whatever you can do, you have to do it effectively if you can identify a guardian. I'm sorry to tell you this, but I think it's still *legitimate*.

To recapitulate my crucial two points. First, bear in mind that violence is *already* here. Because, as I said in my book, *On Violence*, our usual perception is that violence only means change, when something happens. No! Violence is here all the time so that things remain peacefully the way they are. Don't forget about this about violence. And for the second point, don't confuse this elementary violence – let's call it civil disobedience – with brutal physical violence. We can understand an attempt to ignore power as being just for the right of the people when conditions demand it. It's a very forceful weapon – maybe it will become more and more forceful. And you should never forget that the state is not *up there*. The state functions only as far as it is recognized as functioning. I mean, people have tremendous power in organizing themselves just to ignore the power.

For example, in Slovenia – it is not a good example

because it is more opportunistic – I remember we debated how to deal with conscription after independence. People acted spontaneously. When they got a call, young people simply ignored it. They threw the documents away. Police tried to bring in a couple of them, but then it became so massive and the state was confronted with the problem of having to arrest 40,000 people. And of course what they did was a nice humiliating retreat. They disguised it as a change in the law. All of sudden they discovered that it was strategically better for Slovenia to have a small professional army. They quickly changed the law, because people had simply ignored it. Again, if enough people do this, you can have power.

So this is the violence I advocate: *symbolic* violence. For me, one of the greatest critiques of ideology is in the Old Testament, in *The Book of Job*, where God takes the side of Job. The other one is Étienne de La Boétie's *Discours de la servitude volontaire*. He first described the mechanism of how a tyrant becomes a tyrant: because people treat him as a tyrant and fear him. Which is why these magical moments always fascinate me. Even if a leader still nominally holds power, all of a sudden people know that the game is over and don't take it seriously and lose respect, and then a mysterious rupture takes place.

I wrote about it in my early book with a quote from a Polish journalist, Ryszard Kapuściński, who recently died. He wrote a book, *Shah of Shahs*, which was wonderful. It's mainly about the Khomeini revolution and how it took three or four months for the Shah regime to disintegrate at a square in Tehran. At a Tehran crossroad, some protesters refused to budge when a policemen approached them and shouted, "Go away. This is prohibited." One of demonstrators simple stood there and just looked at him. The policeman continued shouting, but the demonstrator didn't move. The embarrassed policeman simply withdrew; in a couple of hours, all Tehran knew about this incident, and although street fights went on for weeks, everyone somehow knew the game was over. This became the symbol of the power of ignoring power.

Is something similar going on now in Egypt? Even if that was happening, people died. But at some level, those in power lost their hold on the people. I think it would be wonderful to do a history of Eastern Europe: the integration of communist regimes at this level. At what point did this magic moment occur even though communists were formally still in power? All of a sudden freedom erupted. This is not just in the sense of intimate freedom, but *social freedom*. And in the sense of symbolic authority, those in power lost it. People were no longer afraid of them. This is a truly magic moment. Why? Because nothing happens in reality; it's not that they stepped down, but in a very mysterious way everyone, even those in power, knows that the game is over. I wouldn't call it a symbol of violence, but this is, for me, the essence of revolution.

I'm not talking about some mystical inner event, because it's a *social* effect. Power no longer works as a social link. When it is said that people are not afraid, it doesn't mean that they are crazily heroic. Of course, if you see a policeman shooting at you, you should be afraid and run away. But at a different level, you no longer take the leadership seriously. Those in power know this is the most dangerous moment for them. This is what Mubarak is now trying to do. This was already happening. And Mubarak's solution was to organize these brutal people to come and start beating, and in this way to create a demand for power. But it failed. So just by ignoring and not being afraid of the authorities, impossible revolution can truly occur.

30

Gandhi, Aristide, and Divine Violence

You concluded your book, In Defense of Lost Causes, *by saying that the domain of pure violence is the domain of love. Here we are thinking of elements that include ethics, universal love, compassion, and empathy. In particular, we are interested to hear your ideas about love and compassion, which we see as a practice of the common good. Alain Badiou sees love as a means to revolution, but you take a different view. What would the practice of the common good look like? You say that revolution cannot happen without cruelty and violence, but you also quote Che Guevara – "At the risk of seeming ridiculous, let me say that the true revolutionary is guided by a great feeling of love. It is impossible to think of a genuine revolutionary lacking this quality" – on the animating role of love in revolution. What do you make of the examples of Gandhi, Mandela, and Aristide as regards the transformative power of love in revolution?*

SŽ: Talking about love, I like to quote Christ, who says: "If anyone comes to me, and does not hate his own father and mother, wife and children, brothers and sisters, yes, and even his own life, he cannot be my disciple" (Luke 14:26). How are we to read this statement?

Love is, for me, a *category of struggle*. For example, I once said, to provoke my friend, that Gandhi was more violent than Hitler. You know what I wanted to say? Of course Hitler was more violent in the sense of killing people. But in reality, all this violence was, in terms of Nietzsche, *reactive*. Basically, Hitler's problem was how to save the capitalist regime, how to prevent revolution. He did not really *act*; all his actions were fundamentally reactions. And he was doing all this just to make things stay the way they had been.

What Gandhi did, although it was very peaceful but in a way extremely violent, was to boycott customs, etc. He targeted the entire structure of the British colonial state. Hitler never did this. He never targeted the functioning of the German state. You see, this is a good example of what I mean by *divine positive violence*. It's just the act of suspending the hold of power.

You mention Nelson Mandela: he was more or less the same. There were of course battles and bombs, but that's another story. Although one must say, in criticism of Mandela and Gandhi, that there's a limit to this procedure. It's very sad. But this procedure, where you play on human dignity, only works, as in Egypt, up to the point where your opponent is minimally dignified *with a certain ethics*.

This is the reason Gandhi's way worked but why you can't universalize it. It worked because the British colonizers, in spite of all the horror, had a certain minimal dignity. Is not the ultimate limitation of Gandhi's strategy, however, that it works only against a liberal democratic regime which abides by certain minimal ethico-political standards – in which, to put it in emotive terms, those in power still "have a conscience"? When Gandhi was asked what the Jews in Germany should do against Hitler in the late 1930s, he said they should commit mass suicide and thus arouse the conscience of the world. But it wouldn't work with the Nazis. We can easily imagine the Nazi reaction to this: "Fine, we'll help you – where do you want the poison delivered to?" This was really tragic.

Do you know about the Truth and Reconciliation Commission (TRC) in South Africa? Here we encounter the inherent limitation of the otherwise sublime effort of the truth and reconciliation strategy in post-apartheid South Africa. It can only work if you can count on minimal ethics. Because do you know what happened a couple of times? It often did work. Do you know what the rule was? Even an evil torturer or a bad guy would come and confront his victims and publicly tell them what he'd done and confess, after which he's pardoned. Anyone who was prepared to tell the truth publicly about his acts, often in front of his or her former victims themselves, was promised clemency, no matter how heinous those acts had been.

But on a couple of occasions some really weird, morally terrifying things happened – for example, the case of the secret police officers who brutally murdered the black activist Steven Biko. The torturer came along and, with a cynical smile, told his story of torture and death in all its grisly details: "Yes, I squeezed your balls, stuck a razor into your mouth . . . Ha-ha, I told you, so now I am free." No remorse, nothing! With a totally shameless person or a cynical subject, this doesn't work.

The ethical horror of this vision is that it displays the limit of the "truth and reconciliation" idea: what if we have a perpetrator for whom the public confession of his crimes not only doesn't give rise to any ethical catharsis in him, but even generates an additional obscene pleasure?

To get back to your question, we always have to see how it works in a certain limited situation. Even Aristide, he also knew when to use violence. Sometimes *defensive* violence is needed. But nonetheless, what we should always remember is that this violence is, in a good sense, *reactive* violence. It should be our basic position, and this is what is so great about identifying an authentic leftist with emancipatory rebellion. You have enemies, but you are never exclusionary. It is love itself that enjoins us to *unplug* ourselves from the organic community into which we were born.

31

No Moralization But Egotism

What will the authentic leftist project be? Is it the moral task, simply evoking utilitarian egotism, or something beyond that? And, as you once mentioned, if there is no need to evoke some high moral ground, then where should it be aiming?

SŽ: In Egypt, for example, you can see that it is an emancipatory demonstration. It's an authentic left because, when the police started to shoot at them, they cried out: "You are with us! You're our brothers! Join us!" Even if they engaged in defensive violence, they didn't stop repeating this message – *join us*. The project is not a murderous one. This project is a positive one.

Here is why the authentic leftist project always distinguishes between *people* and their *functions*: in the same way that we want the end of the bourgeoisie but we don't want to kill all the capitalists. It's a different project. It's always as if, "It's not too late. You have a chance, join us." While fascists are different. Hitler never said to the Jews: "Listen, it was a misunderstanding, join us." No!

For him, Jews were problematic by nature. The only way to solve the problem was to kill them all. This is the huge difference. And it is where the events really confirm this wonderful moment. This is what is so great about the left. Even when they're engaged in struggle, it is an *inclusionary* struggle. It's the struggle with a call: "Join us, you are one of us."

Although fascists claim that they represent all the people, it is obvious they're never able to do so. They always need some kind of external threatening movement, like Jews, foreigners, etc. In other words, they have much more sacrificial logic, as in "Somebody has to be killed."

Then, of course, we know how this works from Rousseau. Rousseau was not an idiot, he wasn't as naive as Marx. In his unique book of dialogues, *Rousseau, Judge of Jean-Jacques*, Rousseau deployed the wonderful idea of distinguishing between two types of egotism – *amour-de-soi* (that love of the self which is natural) and *amour-propre*, the perverted preferring of oneself over others in which a person focuses not on achieving a goal, but on destroying the obstacle to it. Here I wanted to develop a wonderful theory of Rousseau, where he says that egotism is not evil: "The primitive passions, which all directly tend towards our happiness, make us deal only with objects which relate to them, and whose principle is only *amour-de-soi*, are all in their essence lovable and tender; however, when, *diverted from their objects by obstacles, they are more occupied with the obstacle they try to get rid of, than with the object they try to reach*, they change their nature and become irascible and hateful. This is how *amour-de-soi*, which is a noble and absolute feeling, becomes *amour-propre*, that is to say, a relative feeling by means of which one compares oneself, a feeling which demands preferences, *whose enjoyment is purely negative and which does not strive to find satisfaction in our own well-being, but only in the misfortune of others.*"

It's very easy, in contrast to what theologians are saying, to pass from an egotist concern to the common good. He said that we have an assertive egotism, *amour-propre*, and there is nothing bad about that. But he said the problem begins not only when you think that the only way for you to be happy is to hurt others, but when hurting others becomes more important than your own happiness. Here, I totally agree with the criticism over the religious stupidity of the Pope, who says: "Capitalism and egotism, they are both evil." Maybe we don't have *enough* egotism today. No high ethical standards are needed for such a turning point.

What, then, is the logic of envy and resentment? I quoted some Slovene saying – we have all these wonderful proverbs and fairy tales. A magic person asks a farmer what he would prefer: to receive one cow himself while his neighbor receives two cows, or for one of his cows to be killed and two of his neighbor's cows killed. Every Slovenian would prefer the second choice. Better for me to suffer than the neighbor gets more. This logic is crucial when things go wrong, where hurting the other becomes more important even than your own happiness. Gore Vidal demonstrated the point succinctly: "It is not enough for me to win – the other must lose."

That is why I don't think egotism is an evil. An evil person is thus *not* an egotist, he is just "thinking only about his own interests." A true egotist is too busy taking care of his own good to have time to cause misfortune to others. The primary vice of a bad person is precisely that he is more preoccupied with others than with himself. Great philosophers like Hegel and, especially, Schelling knew this. It means elevating yourself above your utilitarian interests and pleasure. This is why the critics complain that, in today's hedonistic-egotistic society, true values totally miss the point. The true opposite of egotist self-love is not altruism, a concern for the common good, but envy, *ressentiment*, which makes me act *against* my own interests. Then evil is very ethical. Evil means: "I will kill you even if I die doing it." It means that you're ready to sacrifice for the hatred of another; you are even ready to sacrifice your own good just to hurt the other.

It's very tragic, I think, how today's religious institutions in Europe are unable to respond to current crises. I think all the answers they give today are simply wrong. What was the response of the Church to the financial crisis? "It is a moral crisis, a crisis of egotism." It's totally wrong. Crisis is in the *system*.

I don't like him, but I almost felt sympathetic toward the horrible guy Bernard Madoff, who stole 60 billion, because he became a scapegoat; everyone blamed him for being a filthy guy. No! He was almost an idealist. As an ideal capitalist today, he took the path where the system pushes you today. The problem isn't Madoff; the problem is *what* pushed him into doing it. How was that possible? It almost sounds anti-Semitic to me. How? Because Madoff was a Jew. When we have these critical moments, I don't like *moralization*, which turns a social process into personal responsibility.

Let us take the case of ecology. We often hear that our ecological crisis is the result of our short-term egotism: obsessed with immediate pleasures and wealth, we forgot about the common good. However, it is here that Walter Benjamin's notion of capitalism as religion becomes crucial: a true capitalist is not a hedonist egotist; he is, on the contrary, fanatically devoted to his task of multiplying his wealth, ready to neglect his health and happiness for it, not to mention the prosperity of his family and the well-being of the environment. There is thus no need to evoke some high-ground moralism and trash capitalist egotism – against capitalist perverted fanatical dedication, it is enough to evoke a good measure of simple egotist and utilitarian concerns. In other words, the pursuit of what Rousseau calls the natural *amour-de-soi* requires a highly civilized level of awareness.

32
Possibility of Concrete Universality

As you said, there is no need to emphasize the importance of identifying hidden assumptions, hidden power claims, in any kind of language of the common good. What do you think would be the most interesting questions around which to organize such a conference? Or if you were putting together discussions with the common good as a key theme, what would be the critical questions that would be worth emphasizing?

SŽ: Here I would like to apply the basic lesson of what Hegel calls *concrete universality*. Universality is never neutral. Whenever you define something as common or neutral or universal – this is a classic Marxist point – it often as a rule secretly privileges some agent. For example, the classic Marxist critique of human rights, the way they've formulated it, already privileges a certain culture or a certain sex, etc.

Some people like to take the idea from Western empires: if you put so much emphasis on individual responsibility, you put less emphasis on social collaboration. Although you claim this as a universal human right, you already privilege a certain Western individualist model – even if you claim they are universal, there's already a certain privilege.

Here is a nice example, which I saw on a history TV program. After the Tiananmen Square demonstration in 1989, the scene was shown repeatedly a million times: one guy alone confronting a tank. But in China, even for those who agreed with the demonstrators, this scene didn't acquire such a symbolic status. It's not a symbol for them. This is a typical Western idea: the military versus one single man. This is not their view. It was a typical example of what they describe as an *icon* – but no! It was an icon for us. It's even a form of racism for them. As Naomi Klein put it in her *Shock Doctrine*, it is doubtful whether the Chinese saw the Tiananmen events as really so profoundly shocking. For them, it wasn't so very symbolic. It's a nice example of how we have to be very careful when constructing universalities.

What further complicates the situation is that the rise of blank spaces in global capitalism is in itself also a proof that capitalism can no longer afford a universal civil order of freedom and democracy, that it increasingly requires exclusion and domination. How are we to break out of the deadlock of post-political dehistoricization? What is to be done after the Occupy Wall Street movement, when the protests which started far away – for example, in the Middle East, Greece, Spain, or the UK – reached the center, and are now reinforced and rolling out all around the world? What should be resisted at this stage is precisely a quick translation of the energy of the protest into a set of *concrete* pragmatic demands.

I do believe in *universalities* like what we see in Egypt and elsewhere. And I think the topic of the secret bias of the common good would be a very good one. You know why? Because I see manipulations on both sides, and by both sides I mean Western Liberals and also the Oriental, Asiatic side. In the West, we should criticize ourselves for privileging this individualist model. But in the East you must know that when they talk about a harmonious society, it often legitimizes suppression. We have here two ways of how we should both engage in *self-criticism*, which almost sounds like Stalinist communism.

In this, I'm almost an old Maoist. Although it sounds very gentle and Confucian, I wonder how much oppression exists in this harmonious hierarchical society. This would be, for me, a true multicultural dialogue. Not the typical boring story of UNESCO reports, which would have argued: "We in the West have our own notions of individuality, and in the East they have notions of an organic harmonious community. We should bring both of them together in a kind of synthesis." No, what we need is exactly the opposite. Where we should collaborate is that each one of us should fight against our own shared experience. We should criticize the bias of our individualism and the bias of the so-called community spirit, which can be exploited to mask oppression.

The standard accusation thus, in a way, knocks at an open door: the whole point of the notion of struggling universality is that true universality and partiality do not exclude one another, but universal *truth* is accessible only from a partially engaged subjective position. What we need to do is take a step away from this external opposition (or mutual reliance) into a direct internalized common ground, which means not only does one pole, when abstracted from the other and thus brought to the extreme, coincide with its opposite, but *there is no primordial duality of poles in the first place, only the inherent gap of the one.* As Schelling, as well as Hegel, remained a monist, so I believe in the possibility of universality. And, as I once mentioned in the book *The Parallax View*, the universal *as such* is the site of an unbearable antagonism, self-contradiction, and the stellar parallax: the traps of ontological difference (the multitude of) its particular species are ultimately nothing but so many attempts to obfuscate/reconcile/master this antagonism. In other words, the universal names the site of a problem-deadlock, of a burning question, and the particulars are the attempted but failed *answers* to this problem.

33
Common Struggle for Freedom

If the question of "concrete universality" is crucial for you, how would you like to transform this idea on a practical level? How can we apply it to the political and social context?

SŽ: I think this question of the common good would be a wonderful topic. You know why? Because you must be aware that your project can easily be appropriated by some kind of New Age spirituality, peace, love, and so on. No! The common good is something of a struggle for me. The common good is a *common struggle for freedom*: not exclusionary struggle, not violent in the sense of shooting or killing, but breaking the hold of those in power. Again, I think, this topic is crucial.

Because everything manipulates. In this respect, Chávez was the same. I'm sorry, but I don't think the Latino American populist model can be universally applied, and I don't think it will ever work for them. I think this will be their ruin. I also don't like this idea of, "Who are you to tell us about our tradition?" This is what the Chinese often say. I think everyone should be allowed to criticize everyone else on the condition that we are also all prepared to be criticized ourselves. What I don't like about the Chinese is that, if you criticize them for lack of freedom, they say, "Oh, you're a racist, you're importing pure imperialist notions!" No, we should be able to criticize everyone. I have the right to criticize your society, and you have the right, too. Why? Because this is very productive.

Let me tell you an anecdote from Hollywood. Many good films that give a critical view on American society are made by immigrant directors from Europe. Sometimes a foreigner who has only a naive view from outside can see much better what is wrong in a society than those who are already living there. Even in Europe, it is the same. This viewpoint could perhaps be designated as that of the Persian ambassador from Montesquieu's famous *Persian Letters*: a strange look upon our world destined to bring about our own estrangement from it. He criticized France through the eyes of a fictional Persian ambassador, who came there and noted many strange things. I think we shouldn't respect each other. But it's important that you include yourself in the game, such that my criticism of you is not a way to elevate myself.

Here I like Descartes, who is often accused of being Eurocentric. There is the famous opening – this could be a wonderful beginning of good multiculturalism – of Chapter 3 of Descartes' *Discourse on Method*, in which he outlines the necessity and content of the "provisory code of morals" that he adopted while engaged in the search for a new unconditional foundation: "The first was to obey the laws and customs of my country, adhering firmly to the faith in which, by the grace of God, I had been educated from my childhood and regulating my conduct in every other matter according to the most moderate opinions ... I was convinced that I could not do better than follow in the meantime the opinions of the most judicious; and although there are some perhaps among the Persians and Chinese as judicious as among ourselves." We should turn Descartes around: infinity can emerge only within the horizon of finitude; it is a category of finitude.

Here is an old phrase I like: "The only way to the universal good is that we all become strangers to ourselves." You imagine looking at yourself with a foreign gaze, through foreign eyes. I think this is something that could be the greatest thing in humanity. You are never really limited just to your own perspective. I don't like the false identity politics of multiculturalism which says that "you are enclosed in your culture." No, we have all this amazing capacity to be surprised, not by others, but by ourselves seeing how what we are doing is strange.

I like this wonderful and simple example: some anthropologists found that, for them, the treasure in a Polynesian island was represented by a big precious stone, which was carved. But then there was an earthquake or storm, and the stone was submerged under water. They didn't have access to it. But they say: "Oh, it's still there even though we can't see it." And we say: "Oh, how stupid they are." But isn't this what we do with gold in Fort Knox? Piles of gold have to lie around uselessly at Fort Knox so that the so-called monetary balance is maintained. It's exactly the same. It's there, inaccessible to us, but it nonetheless functions. I think this is the best multicultural critical anthropology. Where you discover in foreigners what obviously appears to be stupid, but then you find we're doing the same!

This is the *Interpassivity Model*. I'd like to start by making fun of those stupid Tibetans who do not have to pray. The Tibetan praying wheel works like this: I put a piece of paper with a prayer written on it into the wheel, turn it around mechanically (or, even more practically, let the wind turn it around), and the wheel is praying for me – as the Stalinists would have put it, "objectively" I am praying, even if my thoughts are occupied with the most obscene sexual fantasies. To dispel the illusion that such things can only happen in "primitive" societies, think about canned laughter on a TV screen (the reaction of laughter to a comic scene which is included in the soundtrack itself): even if I do not laugh, but simply stare at the screen, tired after a hard day's work, I nonetheless feel relieved after the show, as if the TV did the laughing for me. To grasp this strange process properly, one should supplement the fashionable notion of interactivity, with its uncanny double, interpassivity.

This is the best of critical multiculturalism. You start by making fun of the other. Why not? I like racist jokes. They're the best. We're not making jokes so much about the other; we are basically making jokes about ourselves. I think this is the best way to fight racism. Not to oppress it, but let's say you have a certain racist cliché, you in a playful way accept it and make fun of yourself. I know, it is already a bit out of fashion, about the stupidity of blond girls. And what we all do here, for example – you must know this, I repeat it all the time – here in ex-Yugoslavia, Montenegro people are supposed to be lazy. They make fun of it in a wonderful way.

And people in Bosnia pretend to be so primitive, cheating, and obsessed with sex. They make fun of it all the time. It's a much better approach than politically correct terrorism. It can work.

Even in much of today's progressive politics, the danger is not passivity, but pseudo-activity, the urge to be active and to participate. People intervene all the time, attempting to "do something"; academics participate in meaningless debates. The truly difficult thing is to step back and to withdraw from it. Those in power often prefer even a critical participation to silence – just to engage us in a dialogue, to make sure that our ominous passivity is broken. Against such an interpassive mode in which we are active all the time to make sure that nothing will really change, the first truly critical step is to withdraw into passivity and to refuse to participate. This first step clears the ground for a true activity, for an act that will effectively change the coordinates of the constellation.

Back to your point, this would have been a wonderful topic of how to define the common good by becoming strangers to ourselves. I don't believe the cultural approach taken by the United Nations or UNESCO. The reason that the books they publish in the name of culture, history, and humanity are so boring is that they're terribly afraid of hurting anyone. "What a beautiful civilization here, what a beautiful civilization there." I prefer to look at how stupid they are. And say: "Look, they're even more stupid and so on." That's the only hope.

34
The Impossible Happens

For the final question, what do you consider to be the most urgent theoretical question of our time?

SŽ: There may be two sets of questions. First, there is of course the social question. It is a practical one. After the failure of social democracy, not so much but especially communism, and even after we have clearly seen the limits of direct council and local democracy, how can we imagine *the real alternative?* This is for me the tragedy of all that Seattle protest and Porto Alegre movement. These are protest movements. Everything works well as long as you only protest and then you have the enemy there. I had long debates with different people who are with Porto Alegre. Unlike the way the official slogan puts it, "another world is possible," it seems, instead, that the Porto Alegre reunions have somehow lost their impetus. Just at the moment when there is the possibility of actually taking power, everything explodes. You have on the one hand those who say, "Don't even think about the state, let's think about local democracy," but it's never clear what they mean. Do they mean we should leave the state alone? Or that there should be no state?

In the case of Hardt and Negri, they discern two ways to oppose the global capitalist empire: either the "protectionist" advocacy of the return to the strong nation-state, or the deployment of the even more flexible forms of multitude. Along these lines, in his analysis of the Porto Alegre anti-globalist meeting, Hardt emphasizes the new logic of the political space there. But what about when – if this really is the desire and will of these movements – "we take it over"? What would the "multitude in power" look like? Furthermore, is the state today really withering away (with the advent of the much-praised liberal "deregulation")? On the contrary, isn't the "war on terror" the strongest assertion yet of state authority? Are we not witnessing now the unheard-of mobilization of all (repressive and ideological) state apparatuses?

For me, one of the tragic examples here is the Zapatista movement. I like it, but look at how they got lost. It started with an *ambiguity*. Is it a political movement or just a critical movement? And then, it found a *modus vivendi* by changing itself into a kind of moral authority. Now that it is a threat to no one, everyone simply loves it. Because every politician says: "It's so nice to have these honest people, telling us what to do, but we live in real lives, so somebody has to do the dirty work."

No wonder my radical friend in Mexico once told me about an anonymous boss, Subcomandante Marcos. He said that many Mexican leftists now call him "Subcomediante" Marcos. Because he's the kind of preacher to whom everybody listens because they love him. Even the establishment loves him, because he's a threat to no one. I spoke with a guy who visited there. He told me wonderfully amusing details about how it really is. They have their own small liberated zone. The government doesn't care and leaves them alone because it's good for tourism. Then tourists come there. But there's a problem because they want to be ethical there, so they have no gambling, no prostitution, no alcohol. But the tourists need these things. So Zapatista organized something in the evenings, then, if you want, a bus would take you just outside the liberated zone where you have bordellos, prostitution, alcohol, etc. So you visit the *capitalist vice* soon after you return to communism.

It's not really an alternative. Again, we don't really know what *political model* can replace it. Here I have a big problem with Negri and Hardt: the idea of absolute democracy and *multitude*, I think, doesn't work as a global model. It cannot be universalized. No wonder that, at the end of the second volume of *Multitude*, after describing multiple forms of resistance to the empire, they talk about the final resolution with an almost Messianic note adumbrating the great Rupture, the moment of Decision: "The moment will come when the state will disappear and multitudes will govern themselves." But they don't even give any indication. All of a sudden, they adopt purely religious language, quoting St. Francis of Assisi as a figure of the multitude. These vague analogies and examples simply bring out an anxious suspicion.

More generally, your project would be a concrete political question. But more radically, I think it would be a reasonable attempt, and the following task that I like to explore would be a job for philosophers, not only for scientists. What is happening to us today should be referred to in the context of *being human*. As I mentioned before, all those changes, like bio-genetic manipulations and ecological crisis, are in a way transforming the very definition of being human. We are capable of doing things which will change our very perception of what it means to be human. If we or somebody else could control our physical and psychic properties, we would become much more powerful, but at the same time more subordinated, more vulnerable. It's a very dangerous situation and we don't have any clear ethical guidance here.

And did you notice, when you talk about the possible and the impossible, how strangely this is distributed? On the one hand, in the domains of personal freedom and scientific technology, we are told that "nothing is impossible": we can enjoy sex in all its perverse versions, entire archives of music, films, and TV series are available to download, space travel is available to everyone at a price. There is the prospect of enhancing our physical and psychic abilities, of manipulating our basic properties through interventions into the genome; even the tech-gnostic dream of achieving immortality by transforming our identity into software that can be downloaded into one or another set of hardware. What I'm saying is: everything is possible in technology. They even say that all diseases will be cured. The ultimate dream is the agnostic dream of technology that we will become immortal by changing ourselves into a software program, etc. Here, everything is possible.

But, on the other hand, in the domain of socio-

economic relations, our era perceives itself as the age
of maturity in which humanity has abandoned the
old millenarian utopian dreams and accepted the con-
straints of reality – read: capitalist socioeconomic reality
– with all its impossibilities. When you want to make
some changes to the economy to give a little bit more
for healthcare, they say: "No, it's impossible. The
market won't allow it." We can become immortal, but
we cannot get a little bit more money for healthcare.
The commandment "You cannot" is its *mot d'ordre*.
Obviously, there is something terribly wrong here with
this disposition of *what is possible* and *what is impossible*. So again I think that the task of thinking today
is – maybe to bring these two aspects together and put
them into one abstract problem – to formulate precisely
in a new way to rearrange the limits of the possible and
the impossible.

At certain levels, things we think of as possible are
probably not possible: all those dreams of immortality
or whatever. And at certain levels, what economists are
telling us is impossible is possible. The impossible happens: not impossible in the sense of religious miracles,
but in the sense of something we don't consider possible
within our coordinates. This is why Lacan's formula for
overcoming an ideological impossibility is not "everything is possible," but "the impossible happens." The
Lacanian impossible-real is not an a priori limitation,
which needs to be realistically taken into account, but
the domain of action. An act is more than an interven-
tion into the domain of the possible – an act changes the
very coordinates of what is possible and thus retroac-
tively creates its own conditions of possibility. Like in
Egypt, the impossible happened, no one expected it was

possible. Without clear limitations between the possible and the impossible, you cannot have a minimal stability that is probably needed for normal regular life.

People who just like the events, as in Egypt, used to say that we cannot live in this situation all the time. This is also Mubarak's dirty strategy. He wanted to prolong it and to make things more painful for people ; he expected them to say: "OK, that's enough. Mubarak, come back and give us peace." For me, again, the many reactionaries, today's conservatives at least, like these moments of revolution, but then they say: "The game is over and we must return." But do we really have to return? I think changes are possible.

What is impossible? Our answer should be a paradox which turns around the one with which I began: *soyons réalistes, demandons l'impossible*. The only realist option is to do what appears impossible within this system. This is how the impossible becomes possible.

This is what cynics are telling us: "Yes, we need revolutionary upheaval every 30 years so that people can see that you cannot really change everything in the long term and you must return to the old game." For example, there is no conservative today in France who's point of pride is to say "I was there in '68, and I was demonstrating but later I became a realist." No! One must blur the line between what is possible and what is impossible and *redefine* it in a new way. So this would be for me the great task of thinking today: to *redefine* and *rethink* the limits of the possible and the impossible.